Dinner Party with the Saints

Dinner Party with the Saints

WOODEENE KOENIG-BRICKER

Recipes by Celia Murphy

PARACLETE PRESS
BREWSTER, MASSACHUSETTS

2021 First Printing

Dinner Party with the Saints

Copyright © 2021 by Woodeene Koenig-Bricker

ISBN 978-1-64060-419-3

The Paraclete Press name and logo (dove on cross) are trademarks of Paraclete Press.

Library of Congress Cataloging-in-Publication Data
Names: Koenig-Bricker, Woodeene, 1952- author.
Title: Dinner party with the saints / Woodeene Koenig-Bricker; recipes by
  Celia Murphy.
Description: Brewster, Massachusetts : Paraclete Press, 2021. | Summary:
  "Combining fictional narrative, fascinating biographies of sixteen.
  saints, and mouth-watering dinner party recipes, the book offers a
  resource to celebrate saints spanning the history of the Church"--
  Provided by publisher.
Identifiers: LCCN 2020032424 (print) | LCCN 2020032425 (ebook) | ISBN
  9781640604193 | ISBN 9781640604209 (mobi) | ISBN 9781640604216 (epub) |
  ISBN 9781640604223 (pdf)
Subjects: LCSH: Dinners and dining--Religious aspects--Catholic Church. |
  Christian saints--Miscellanea. | Cookbooks.
Classification: LCC BR115.N87 K64 2021 (print) | LCC BR115.N87 (ebook) |
  DDC 270.092/2--dc23
LC record available at https://lccn.loc.gov/2020032424
LC ebook record available at https://lccn.loc.gov/2020032425

10 9 8 7 6 5 4 3 2 1

Published by Paraclete Press
Brewster, Massachusetts
www.paracletepress.com

Digitally printed

For Pippa

CONTENTS

INTRODUCTION

*W*elcome to a Dinner Party with the Saints! Pull up a chair and join a select group of the Heavenly Host as we celebrate their lives . . . and some special foods.

Why a dinner party? One of the traditional images of heaven is the Banquet or Marriage Feast of the Lamb. Revelation 19:9 says, "Blessed are those who called to the wedding feast of the Lamb." The idea of those who have lived a holy life, gathering in celebration, has often been interpreted as our being present at the Eucharist with all those saints in heaven. But what if the banquet could be seen as a little more earthly than theological? In this book, I imagine what it would be like if sixteen saints were to gather for a dinner party in heaven as they await the arrival of the Guest of Honor.

For far too long, the stories of the saints have emphasized their spirituality instead of their personalities. How often have you read the hagiography of a saint that could be summarized as "He or she did good deeds, helped the poor, prayed a lot, accepted suffering, and died a holy death." Now, of course, the reason they are saints is because of their good deeds, help for the poor, writings, and prayers, but sometimes in emphasizing their spirituality, we lose sight of the people who lived and breathed and loved—and slept and laughed and ate—in a specific time and place in history.

Another, more modern temptation in telling the lives of saints is to abandon the hagiography for pure history. This is just as insidious, since a biography often seeks to undercover faults and failures, often with more than a soupçon of judgment. In doing so, the flaws that are part of all humanity can take precedence over the striving for holiness, and we are left wondering exactly why the person was considered to be so holy. Not to mention the fact that we are often tempted to judge their actions by the psychological understandings of our own times and think that the saints may have been more in need of therapy than canonization.

In this book, my desire is that you will get to know the saints in a new and hopefully entertaining way by seeing them interacting in an imaginary setting, but while still being the very real men and women they were and still are.

Naturally, I've had to take major liberties, because the conversations and activities surrounding the party are purely figments of my imagination. For those of you who are scholars and students of a certain saint, I'm sure you will feel that I left out many important details. To that, I say that this is not to be taken as a scholarly record of any of the saints represented here. This is not a "lives of the saints." The biographies are meant to be a sampling of their lives, not a comprehensive study. However, the actual biographical material and historical facts are as accurate as I can make them. And because the stories and legends about them are often great fun to read, I've included a sampling of the tales that have been told about them. These are to be taken with a "grain of salt."

But the foods they bring are based, as much as possible, on ingredients and foods that they either talked about eating or would have eaten in their historical periods. My dear friend Celia Murphy, who is classically trained in culinary arts, helped me create the recipes. (Okay, she created them. I just gave historical guidelines and encouragement. Except for the locusts. I figured them out on my own.) With her masterful touch, they are designed for modern cooks and modern palates, including vegetarian and gluten-free options. I'd like to think that the saints would recognize and enjoy the food even if they didn't have the exact same dishes on their tables.

My hope is that you will enjoy sitting down at this *Dinner Party with the Saints* and come away with a deeper appreciation for these holy people, as well as a few moments of amusement and several great recipes to try. If so, then I will feel greatly blessed indeed.

Dinner Party with the Saints

CHAPTER 1
St. Peter

So what else do you need for the dinner party?" St. Peter asked, while ticking names off a list resting on the counter of the checkpoint for heaven. He looked up and waved through the Pearly Gates a wide-eyed man clutching a small child. The man and his infant son were still dripping from the tsunami that had claimed their lives moments before. A piece of seaweed dangled over the child's face. "Make sure they get dried off," Peter said to the angel standing at attention near him. "And see that the baby gets a nice toy." The angel nodded, his placid features at odds with the flaming sword in his hands. "Now then," Peter said, turning to a petite dark-haired woman with flashing brown eyes tapping her foot impatiently. "The party."

"Yes, the party," St. Teresa of Avila said. "I think we've got it covered." She checked off items using her fingers. "Guests invited. Room set up. At least we know there won't be a problem with weather," she laughed.

"Well, St. Brigit might like a little rain," Peter said. "She did come from a rainy part of the world."

"Too bad," Teresa said. "After that little donkey and stream incident, I'm happy never to see another drop of rain."

"Donkey and stream?"

"I thought everyone knew that story," she said.

Peter shook his head. "I must have missed it."

"I was traveling to visit one of my convents," Teresa began. "The weather had been frightful, and the bridge was washed out over one of the streams we had to cross. I decided to ride the donkey, but he panicked and we both ended up being swept downstream. I was soaked to the skin, everything in the cart was lost, and I don't mind telling you, I was pretty annoyed with God." Peter raised an eyebrow. "I remember saying, 'If this is how you treat your friends, it's no wonder you have so few of them,'" Teresa added.

"And what reply did you get?"

"The only one I expected. Just a sort of chuckle that could have been distant thunder."

"Sounds about right," Peter added.

"But enough about me," Teresa said. "Are you going to be with us? I know you are one of the busiest saints up here, tending the Golden Gate and all."

"Pearly gates," Peter corrected. "Fortunately, we aren't bound by the laws of time and space," he replied. "I can be in two places at once if need be. As you know, when saints used to do that on earth—bilocation, I think it's called—it really freaked people out; but up here, it's par for the course."

"Do you even know what that expression means?" Teresa teased.

"It means you've played a round of golf with an average, ordinary score. Nothing special. Brigit told me," Peter said as he waved another soggy group into heaven. "Golf was invented in her part of the world. A bit after her time, and in Scotland, not Ireland, but she has always been interested in things of Celtic origin. You can take the girl out of the Celts, but you can never take the Celtic out of the girl. Or so I've been told. Anyway, I think I might have liked playing golf. Out in the fresh air, walking, being with friends. Maybe we should consider building a course up here."

Teresa rolled her eyes. "Chasing a little white ball. What a waste of time. But each to their own, I suppose. I think fishing is boring, too." She watched as Peter waved through another family who had been taken by the tsunami.

"It's going to get pretty busy here in a few minutes," Peter said. "Natural disasters and wars always make for a lot of new arrivals. But I'll be there as soon as I can."

"So, what have you been assigned to bring to the dinner party?" Teresa asked abruptly. "Something good, I hope."

Peter smiled wryly. "Fish . . . and bread."

"Of course. We couldn't have a banquet without them. How many fish are you going to bring? Two?" she asked, with a glint in her eye.

"Enough for all," Peter said with a wry smile. "There is always enough since it's easier to multiply up here than it was down there. What about you? I know you have a bit of a sweet tooth."

"Not this time," Teresa said, "but I have a special treat planned. Speaking of which, I need to check on it. Wouldn't want it to get overdone. When are you going to come?" she asked, as she pushed open the guardhouse door and let the celestial light flood in.

"Soon. I'll be busy here for a while longer, but I do have to escort the guest of honor to the feast."

"Only fitting, since you are the rock on which the Church was built. I'll see you both when you get there."

Peter smiled and then turned to the increasingly long line of new arrivals. Their names kept appearing on the sheets in front of him—a bit of quantum physics disguised as magic, he liked to say. After a lifetime of physical activity as a fisherman, he rather liked tending the Pearly Gates.

He enjoyed seeing the look of surprise on some people's faces as they realized where they had ended up. He especially enjoyed seeing those who had been skeptical or even disbelievers in their lives realize that there really was an afterlife—and it was good.

Peter felt a tiny frisson of what he vaguely remembered as anxiety as he looked at all the tsunami victims. Drowning had been one of his greatest fears when he was on earth.

The Greek word that we generally translate as "fisherman" is more akin to "seaman." It is a general term for anyone who made their living on or near the sea, such as a longshoreman or a sailor, rather than a specific career designation. However, we do know that Peter and his brother Andrew were actual fishermen since they were catching fish in nets.

• •

It is unlikely that Peter knew how to swim since, as odd as it seems to us, fishermen and sailors of that time often did not know how. This would explain why Peter was so panicked when he began to sink as he walked on water toward Jesus.

He supposed he could take swimming lessons in his spare time, but that would require getting wet, and he had been wet enough all the times he had waded in the Sea of Galilee for another few millennia.

The Sea of Galilee, where Peter spent his time, is not a sea, but is actually a large lake. Roughly thirteen miles long and eight miles wide, it rests about 680 feet below sea level and has a maximum depth of 150 feet. Other names for this body of water include Lake Gennesaret, Sea of Tiberias, and Chinnerth. Today it is called the Sea of Kinneret, and it is Israel's largest source of drinking water.

The line of people wound back and forth, seemingly to the horizon if there were such a thing in heaven. Processing that many people would take weeks, maybe even months on earth, but here in heaven, everyone felt as if they were tended to immediately. It was one of the nicest things about the celestial heights. No waiting.

Peter picked up the paper with an ever-increasing number of names appearing on it. "Welcome," he said opening his arms to another wet group that was huddling together. "We've been expecting you."

Did You Know?

At the time of St. Peter, the pyramids of Egypt were already nearly 3,000 years old!

St. Peter

UNKNOWN – AD 64

The story of St. Peter is part and parcel of the foundation of Christianity. The rough and tumble fisherman was among the first followers of Jesus, and his journey of faith took him from the shores of the Sea of Galilee to Vatican Hill in Rome, where, according to tradition, he was martyred.

Simon, son of Jonah, was from Bethsaida but lived in Capernaum, where he and his brother Andrew ran a fishing business.

They apparently were successful enough to have owned their own fishing boat and have at least two employees, James and John.

Andrew was originally a disciple of John the Baptist. After Andrew concluded Jesus was the Messiah, he told this to Simon, and Simon gave up his fishing business to follow Jesus. We know that Peter was married, but we do not have any record as to what his wife thought about his new career path. Although it would be unlikely that she, if she were still living, would have actually taken up the nets herself, she might well have continued to run the apparently prosperous business with other employees since Peter was able to return to his boat after the Crucifixion. After the Crucifixion, in John 21:3, he told Thomas, Nathanael, and four other disciples in a phrase that still expresses

Both Bethsaida and Capernaum, now archaeological sites, are located on the northern shore of the Sea of Galilee.

• •

Because wood was such a scarce and treasured commodity, wooden fishing boats were highly prized and carefully repaired. The remains of one such boat, known as the Jesus Boat, was found in 1986 when drought exposed it on the shore of the Sea of Galilee. While there is no evidence it is Peter's boat, it is very similar to the ones Peter would have owned.

• •

Fishermen in Peter's time often fished at night because their nets were less visible to fish in the darkness.

his clear frustration, "I am going fishing." It was at that time, after a disappointing night on the lake, that Jesus appeared to them, telling them to let down their nets one last time.

At one point, Jesus changed Simon's name to Peter, a name meaning rock or stone. Jesus then said that it was upon this rock that he would build his Church, thus indicating that Peter was to become the leader of the Twelve Apostles.

Peter was present at all of the major events of Jesus's ministry, including the Transfiguration, as well as most of Jesus's most notable miracles such as the Feeding of the Five Thousand. He himself experienced the net-breaking haul of fish as recorded in Luke 5:1–11 as well as walking (at least temporarily) on water.

There are about twenty different kinds of fish in the Sea of Galilee. The most famous is the Tilapia Galilea, sometimes called St. Peter's Fish. It was the most commonly consumed fish in Peter's time. Sardines, referred to as "small fish," may have been the fish used in the multiplication of the loaves and fish. Another fish found in the Sea of Galilee is called *sfamnun*, in Hebrew. A type of catfish, it was considered unclean according to Jewish dietary law because of its lack of scales and thus was unlawful to consume. Because *sfamnun* has an eel or snakelike appearance, some scholars think that Jesus might have been referring to it rather than a true serpent when he said that no good father would give his child a snake when asked for a fish (Luke 11:11).

At the Last Supper, Peter famously refused to let Jesus wash his feet until Jesus explained that if he didn't permit it, Peter would have "no part with me." That made the ever-impetuous Peter tell Jesus to wash his feet and his hands and his head as well. Despite his affirmations of faith, Peter denied Jesus three times before the Crucifixion, leading to his great sorrow. However, his remorse wasn't enough for him to actually attend the Crucifixion; instead he went into hiding.

After Mary Magdalene and the other women told the Apostles that Jesus had been raised from the dead, Peter and John ran to the empty tomb, where Peter saw the linen burial wrappings as well as the cloth that had been placed on Jesus's head, even though he did not fully understand what had happened. Following Pentecost and his infusion of courage, Peter traveled extensively, spreading the gospel. He journeyed to Lydda, Joppa, Caesarea, Samaria, Antioch, and possibly Corinth while making numerous trips back to Jerusalem where, along with James the Just and John, he was revered as an elder of the faith.

Although Paul does not mention Peter by name in any of his writings, tradition says that the two men worked together in Rome, with Peter serving as the city's first bishop. It has long been believed that Peter was crucified in the gardens of Nero shortly after the fire that destroyed Rome in AD 64. According to tradition, he was crucified upside down, so as not to die exactly like Jesus, and was buried under what is now the high altar of the Basilica of St. Peter. In the 1960s, bones from a man in his sixties were located where tradition had always placed them, causing Pope Paul VI to declare they were most likely the relics of Peter.

Two epistles in the New Testament have been attributed to Peter. Because of the sophisticated use of Greek, some scholars question if Peter himself wrote the letters, since it would be unusual for an Aramaic-speaking fisherman to have studied classical Greek. One likely suggestion is that Peter may have used a secretary to assist him, as did Paul. The letters themselves are primarily concerned with encouraging Christians to stay steadfast even in the light of persecution and do not contain any new doctrine or dogma. Several other apocryphal writings have been attributed to Peter or claim to quote him, including the Gospel of Mary and the Acts of Peter.

The idea that Peter would be the gatekeeper of heaven is based on Matthew 16:19 in which Jesus says, "I will give you the keys to the kingdom of heaven. Whatever you bind on earth shall be bound in heaven; and whatever you loose on earth shall be loosed in heaven." While traditional Catholic teaching has often cited this passage with regard to the Sacrament of Reconciliation, it has also been used to suggest that Peter uses his keys to admit souls to heaven.

St. Peter is the patron of many professions including, obviously enough, locksmiths, fishermen, and shipbuilders, but also butchers, bakers, and cobblers, the latter because he walked on water with Jesus. He is remembered on June 19, the Feast of Saints Peter and Paul.

Legends, Lore, and Miracles

It is known that Peter was married, since Jesus healed his mother-in-law (Matt. 8:14–15), and Paul refers to Peter's wife in 1 Corinthians 9:5, although she is never named. Eusebius, a Roman historian, says she was martyred the same day as Peter. Legend says that they had a daughter named Petronilla who also died a martyr's death. Certain families in modern-day Syria and Lebanon claim direct blood lineage to him.

The apocryphal Acts of Peter recounts the story that when Peter was fleeing Rome to avoid execution, he met the risen Lord. Peter asked Jesus, "*Quo vadis?*" or, "Where are you going?" Jesus replied, "I am going to Rome to be crucified again." This gave Peter the courage to turn back and face his martyrdom.

Peter is said to have preached and taught in the catacomb of St. Priscilla on the Via Salaria in Rome.

One of the oldest representations of Peter is on a bronze medallion from the third century. Throughout the ages, the image of Peter has been singularly consistent, showing a stocky, bearded man with curly hair.

Peter, along with Paul, is said to have appeared to Attila the Hun in the fifth century, dissuading him from sacking the city of Rome. St. Peter Nolasco (1189–1256) claimed that Peter appeared to him to encourage him to continue his missionary work in Spain.

Quote
"Master, to whom shall we go? You have the words of eternal life."
(John 6:68)

Recipe

St. Peter would have caught and eaten tilapia on a regular basis. Most likely, it would have been grilled over a charcoal fire, as mentioned in John 21:9. It would also have been smoked and dried, resulting in something like fish jerky. On special occasions, tilapia would have been oven-baked and served with herbs and spices. A flavorful herbed crust on top of fresh tilapia fillets in this dish makes for an easy, elegant meal. This parsley-crumb topping is versatile, and is wonderful on lamb and chicken as well.

Parmesan and Parsley-Crusted Roasted Tilapia

- **PREP TIME:** 15 minutes
- **COOK TIME:** 10-15 minutes
- **SERVES:** 6
- **SPECIAL EQUIPMENT NEEDED:** Baking pan (cookie sheet)
- **THIS RECIPE IS LACTO-PESCATARIAN.** It contains fish and cheese.
- **MAKE IT GLUTEN-FREE** by substituting gluten-free breadcrumbs. Or toast several slices of gluten-free bread, then scrape with a grater to make your own gluten-free breadcrumbs. Ensure that your cheese is gluten-free.

INGREDIENTS

6 tilapia fillets, rinsed, patted dry. (If frozen filets are being used, thawed.)

1 cup plain breadcrumbs

1 cup fresh parsley, packed: leaves washed, stems removed (Italian Flat Parsley or Curly Parsley, approximately 1.2 ounces of parsley leaves)

¼ cup Parmesan cheese, grated

¼ cup olive oil, plus extra tablespoon for pan

2 cloves garlic

1 tablespoon fresh lemon juice

¼ teaspoon oregano

½ teaspoon basil

2 teaspoons paprika

¼ teaspoon salt

¼ teaspoon pepper

DIRECTIONS

Preheat oven to 400 degrees.

- If using a food processor:
Place garlic in a food processor with a steel blade. Pulse until finely minced. Add remaining ingredients (except tilapia). Pulse until the parsley is chopped and ingredients are combined.
- Alternate method if not using a food processor: Finely chop the garlic. Finely chop the parsley leaves. In a bowl, add breadcrumbs, Parmesan cheese, salt, pepper, and seasonings. Mix to combine. Add olive oil and stir well until breadcrumbs are coated uniformly. Add lemon juice, garlic, and chopped parsley. Stir well.
- Oil the baking sheet with a tablespoon of olive oil.
- Place tilapia filets on baking sheet, spaced evenly.
- With clean hands, remove ⅙ of the parsley/crumb mixture from bowl and mound evenly onto a filet, patting the topping lightly onto filet.
- Bake for approximately 10-12 minutes, until the thickest part of the filet flakes well with a fork and crumb topping is lightly browned.

Prayers

TRADITIONAL PRAYER

O Holy Apostle, because you are the Rock upon which Almighty God has built His Church, obtain for me I pray you: lively faith, firm hope, and burning love, complete detachment from myself, contempt of the world, patience in adversity, humility in prosperity, recollection in prayer, purity of heart, a right intention in all my works, diligence in fulfilling the duties of my state of life, constancy in my resolutions, resignation to the will of God and perseverance in the grace of God even unto death; that so, by means of your intercession and your glorious merits, I may be made worthy to appear before the Chief and Eternal Shepherd of Souls, Jesus Christ, Who with the Father and the Holy Spirit, lives and reigns forever. Amen.

CONTEMPORARY PRAYER

St. Peter, help me to be able to admit my faults as you did and to be brave enough to make bold changes in my life. Be with me as I face my fears and remind me that, with faith, I, too, can walk on water. Amen.

CHAPTER 2

St. Teresa of Avila

Teresa Sánchez de Cepeda y Ahumada, better known as St. Teresa of Avila, turned away from the Pearly Gates and began walking, no, waltzing, down the golden street that transected the heart of heaven. Even while she lived in sixteenth-century Spain, she loved to dance, and now she danced with abandon, up and down every street in heaven. She had long since given up being "discalced" or barefoot as she did when she was on earth and instead wore high-heeled dance shoes.

"The better to tango!" she liked to say. Today she was wearing bright red boots with blue embroidery on the toes. *I should have shown them to St. Peter,* she thought, remembering that Peter was the patron of cobblers, among other things.

Teresa may not have actually gone barefoot all the time, especially not on her long journeys. She was, after all, as practical as she was spiritual.

• •

Most days she preferred to wander in the distant corners of the heavenly realm, but today she wanted to take the most direct route, so she headed straight down the golden street, turned left at the silver road, and headed toward the electrum path that led to one of the more bucolic corners of heaven.

In ancient times, electrum, an alloy of silver and gold, was one of the most valuable of metals. The Great Pyramid was topped with an electrum summit.

• •

She pushed open the heavy wooden door to her heavenly home—she jokingly called it her "Exterior Castle"—and was immediately greeted by the welcoming aroma of roasting partridge.

Teresa's most famous written work was entitled *The Interior Castle.*

She stopped and took a long, deep breath, savoring the rich, spicy scent. The kitchen was next to the library, a very convenient location, she always said, since food and books went so well together. A staircase next to the kitchen wound its way to a turret overlooking a broad expanse of lawn and garden.

Teresa sighed with pleasure as she thought of the herbs she had picked there to season the partridges.

After opening the oven door and nodding approvingly at the brown glaze forming on the birds, she plopped down in an overstuffed chair in the library and glanced at the stack of books on a table. A romance. A history of fashion. A prayer book. All were well read.

Teresa was fond of fashion and fashionable clothes in her youth and read the equivalent of fashion magazines. She also loved to read romances, which consisted mostly of stories of knights, and even tried writing a few herself. She felt that a day when she couldn't read a new book was a day lost.

• •

Gardens in the 1500s were both functional and decorative. Laid out in rectangular plots, the gardens contained plants that could be used in cooking, for medicine, and simply for pleasure. Kitchen gardens often included fennel, cabbage, onion, garlic, leeks, radishes, parsnips, peas, lentils, and beans. Infirmary gardens might contain savory, fenugreek, rosemary, peppermint, rue, iris, sage, bergamot, mint, fennel, and cumin. Grapes, roses, rosemary, carnations, and jasmine were planted for their beauty and fragrance.

She finally picked up a gardening book with flowers pressed in its pages. She paused for a moment on a design for a moonlit garden, one that consisted entirely of night-flowering and white plants. She made a mental note to ask Martin de Porres about white bougainvillea, a plant native to Peru, the next time they met. *White bougainvillea would be quite striking over a trellis*, she thought. Once, a new arrival to the heavenly realms asked her why she bothered with getting her hands and knees dirty in the soil when all she had to do was will for a garden and one would appear. "Ah," Teresa said. "It's clear you never were a gardener. It's not the having of a completed garden that matters. It's the planning and the planting and tending. A garden is a journey, not a destination. It's just that here we don't have to work as hard to make sure the plants thrive!"

About twenty minutes later, a bell in the kitchen went off. "Done!" she said to herself. "Just in time."

Waiting for chapel bells to signal the end of prayer time used to give her a headache, although headaches weren't a concern of hers anymore.

She pulled the pan of roasted partridge from the oven. Partridge was one of her favorite meals and a fitting dish for a dinner party with an honored guest. Teresa smiled to herself as she poured the fig sauce she had made, remembering a time when a basket of figs was given her as a gift. She sent a few to her brother with a note that if he wasn't going to eat them, he should send them back because she liked them better than he did. She tucked a brilliant white cloth over the top of her dinner party offering and set off down the street of gold.

Moments later, she was standing at the door of a small, rustic cottage with a thatched roof and window boxes filled with flowers of every unimaginable color.

Teresa sometimes found it hard to pray for long periods, often waiting impatiently for the bell that signaled the end of prayer time to ring. She once remarked that the end of the prayer hour could never come fast enough.

• •

It is believed that Teresa suffered from migraines, since her descriptions of auras and lights match those given by migraine sufferers. She is the patron of those who suffer from headaches.

While the building seemed unsuitably small for a dinner party, Teresa knew that looks were deceiving in heaven. The most modest building could house the most magnificent salon and the most disheveled person could be among the most honored of guests. Teresa knocked at the door, listening to the hollow echo. No response. She knocked again. Again, no response. She knocked a third time, this time a little harder. Things tended to work in threes up here—honoring the Trinity and all. A shuffling sound, like someone walking in oversized sandals, came from behind the rough wooden door. She sighed a bit impatiently and shifted the basket on her arm. The smell of cooked fowl wafted upwards and Teresa tucked the covering towel closer to keep in the heat. A breathless panting made her turn to see a ginger-haired woman clad in rough-spun wool charging up the path behind her. "Sorry I'm late," she gasped, as she slid to a stop next to Teresa.

"Oh, St. Brigit, I don't think you're late," Teresa said. "I've been waiting here for several minutes, and no one has come to the door." Just then, a slight creaking noise caught their attention. A beaming, bearded face poked through the opening. "Welcome, welcome! Come on in!" Bl. Solanus Casey pushed the door open and gestured into an amazingly expansive room.

A long table was set with white linen and gleaming gold dishes. Place cards indicated the seating arrangements. Teresa tried not to be too obvious as she looked for her name. "Order of entry," Solanus said, his gray beard bobbing. "The first shall be last and the last shall be first, you know. I think you're over there"—he pointed near the middle of the table. "Now, let's see what you've brought for the party." He lifted the towel and sniffed appreciatively. "Partridge, I'm guessing."

Teresa nodded. "With fig sauce."

Once a nobleman served Teresa and her nuns a meal of partridge. Her nuns were shocked as she tucked in with delight, taking a whole partridge for herself. When questioned, she said, "There is a time for penance and time for partridge and now is the time for partridge."

• •

Spanish Rioja wine has been popular since the eleventh century BC.

"Excellent, excellent!" Solanus clapped his hands in anticipation. "And dear Brigit, I'm sure you must have brought beer."

"Indeed, I have," Brigit said, holding up the jug. "It wouldn't be a proper party without a glass or two of beer, now would it?" Teresa smiled wryly. Beer wasn't her beverage of choice. She was more of a Rioja girl.

Did You Know?

St. Teresa was one of the first two women Doctors of the Church. She and St. Catherine of Siena were granted the title in 1970.

St. Teresa of Avila
MARCH 28, 1515 – OCTOBER 15, 1582

Teresa was born in Avila, Spain. Her grandfather was a Jew who had been forced to convert to Christianity, and her father was a wealthy wool merchant who bought his way into Spanish high society. Raised by devout parents, Teresa was intrigued by the lives of the saints, and when she was seven, she even tried to run away with her brother Rodrigo to experience martyrdom at the hands of the Moors. After their uncle found them and returned them home, Rodrigo put all the blame on Teresa—something she never denied.

When she was about thirteen (some biographies say eleven; others fourteen), her mother died in childbirth, an event that marked Teresa for the rest of her life. She begged the Virgin Mary to become her mother and later said that from that time on, she "never prayed to the Virgin in vain." Although she experienced an early zeal for spirituality, during her adolescence Teresa thoroughly enjoyed the perks of wealth and society. She loved to read romantic stories about knights and was deeply interested in fashion—and boys. Nonetheless, she had spells where she thought of herself as a "miserable sinner," which her father probably thought she was, given his propensity for maintaining exacting standards of behavior.

Her father became concerned about her future, not just because of her fondness for the pleasures of the day, but because of her Jewish heritage. It would have been difficult to find a suitable husband because her grandfather had been Jewish, so her father opted to send her to a convent when she was sixteen. It's not clear if he intended her to remain there for life or just until he exhausted her marriage prospects, but in any event, his mind was made up.

Apparently, she wasn't all that keen on the idea until she found a Carmelite convent that had a particularly relaxed idea of what religious life meant. In fact, some scholars think that the convent might have been more liberal than her father's household.

Although she began as a lay boarder, she gradually began to embrace a more genuinely pious life, at least in part because of an extensive reading of mystical ascetic works and St. Augustine's *Confessions*. Contributing to her conversion was a severe illness, probably malaria, that left her nearly incapacitated. While recuperating, Teresa began to develop a deep mental prayer life, although she continued to have difficulty sitting through extended prayer. After several years of on-again, off-again illness, during which she spent time both at home and in the convent, she eventually recovered, a blessing she attributed to the intercession of St. Joseph.

Saint Teresa is the subject of Bernini's sculpture *The Ecstasy of St. Teresa*, located in Santa Maria della Vittoria, Rome, which commemorates the seraph piercing her heart. She also is said to have been the inspiration for Tess in *Tess of the d'Urbervilles* by Thomas Hardy.

• • • • • • • • • • • • • • • • • • • •

When Teresa first built a convent, she is said to have ordered piles of hay, thinking that at least her nuns would have some place to sleep. Sleeping on hay is the origin of the phrase "hit the hay." It refers to pounding straw to make sure no vermin is nesting in the bedding.

Her spiritual life remained uneven until, at about thirty-nine, she was able to corral her restless spirit and embrace deep contemplation and meditation. On June 29, 1559, she experienced the first of many visions of Jesus. In one, she felt a seraph pierce her heart with a pain that was both agonizing and sweet. Unfortunately, many people felt that her visions were from the devil, not God. This being the time of the Spanish Inquisition, visionaries were sometimes burned at the stake, so Teresa tried to keep her mystical experiences secret. This became more difficult when she reportedly began to levitate during them and had to ask her sisters to hold her down. Nonetheless, the visions continued.

As she entered middle age, she became more dissatisfied with the laxity of religious life in her convent. With the aid of a wealthy friend, she began a project of establishing "reformed" Carmelite convents that would observe stricter rules of poverty and penance.

Because she wanted devout men to be able to experience this same reform, she enlisted the aid of two Carmelite friars, one of whom was St. John of the Cross, to build men's monasteries. Despite her focus on living a simple life, Teresa was not dour. She would often play the tambourine and even danced on tabletops while playing the castanets, an activity that sometimes drew the disapproval of other, more reserved nuns. It was during this time that she wrote her most famous book, *The Interior Castle*, which describes the soul as a castle that must pass through seven "mansions" of prayer on its way to God.

Her reforms did not always go as smoothly as she might have hoped. She was opposed by some Carmelites who disputed her ideas of austerity, and she was forced to "retire" for a time to a convent in Toledo. Being a woman of great resolve, she appealed to the King of Spain and got her "sentence" lifted. She continued to found convents until the end of her life. Eventually, she founded sixteen convents over twenty years.

She died on one of her travels, and her last words are said to be, "My Lord, it is time to move on. Well then, may your will be done. O my Lord and my Spouse, the hour that I have longed for has come. It is time to meet one another."

Because of her vast library of mystical writings, as well as her personal devotion, she was canonized in 1622. In 1970, Pope Paul VI declared her to be the first woman Doctor of the Church, a distinction given to saints who have made a profound contribution to theological thought. Her feast day is October 15, and she is the patron of headache sufferers and writers.

Legends, Lore, and Miracles

One miracle attributed to Teresa involved her nephew Gonzalez. The child was playing at the construction site of one of Teresa's convents when a wall fell and crushed him. Teresa picked up the dead boy, prayed over him, and restored him to life before handing him to his mother. This miracle was cited at her canonization.

Tradition claims Teresa had a particular devotion to the Infant Jesus of Prague and that the statue in the Discalced Carmelite Church of Our Lady Victorious in Malá Strana in Prague belonged to her. The story goes that she gave it to a noblewoman who was traveling to Prague.

She is said to have sent an image of the Immaculate Conception with a brother emigrating to Peru. The image is now located at the Shire of El Viejo in Nicaragua. Much of her body rests in Avila, but her right foot is in Rome, her left hand is in Lisbon, her left eye and right hand are in Ronda, her left arm and heart at in Alba De Tormes, and one finger is in Paris.

Quote
"Just being a woman is enough for my wings to fall off.**"**

Recipe

Roast Partridge (or Hens) with Fig Sauce

Teresa and her nuns would have eaten plain foods including coarse bread, vege-
table stew, and seasonal fruits. Meat would have been a luxury, although cheese
and eggs would have appeared on the table. This recipe honors Teresa's famous
quote about penance and partridges, as well as her documented love for figs.

- **PREP TIME:** 15-20 minutes
- **COOK TIME:** 45 minutes if making sauce while roasting the partridges/hens. Otherwise, approximately 45 minutes to roast birds, and approximately 25 minutes for sauce.
- **SERVES:** 4
- **NOTES:** This recipe works equally well with Rock Cornish Game Hens.
- **SPECIAL EQUIPMENT NEEDED:** A sieve to strain sauce (optional), pan with a lid to cook bacon, then sauce. Roasting pan for birds. Helpful: a quick-check thermometer or roasting thermometer.

INGREDIENTS

4 whole partridges (or Rock
   Cornish Game Hens)
   prepared for roasting
4 slices bacon
1 shallot, chopped
1 tablespoon olive oil
1 clove garlic, crushed
¼ pound dried Mission Figs
   (or any dried figs), stems
   removed, cut into quarters

Juice of 2 oranges, reserve the
   rinds.
2 cups red wine
1 tablespoon balsamic vinegar
   or apple cider vinegar
1 tablespoon honey
1 bay leaf
A few sprigs fresh thyme
Salt and pepper

DIRECTIONS

Preheat oven to 375 degrees.

- Cook the bacon in pan over medium heat. Remove bacon from the pan and set on paper towels to drain. Pour the bacon fat into the bottom of the roasting pan you will be using to cook your partridges.
- Remove any giblets from poultry cavities. Rinse your poultry well under cold water, inside and out, and pat dry with paper towel. Be sure there are no feathers on bird. If so, remove them by pinching feathers tightly between our thumb and pointer finger and pulling, or use kitchen tweezers. Season the outside and cavity lightly with salt and pepper. Place orange rinds in cavity of birds (cut rinds into enough pieces to divide between birds).
- Place birds in roasting pan breast-side up. Spoon some bacon fat from the roasting pan onto birds until covered. Tuck the wing tips underneath birds or cover with foil to protect them from burning. Roast the birds for 45 minutes, basting occasionally. They are done when temperature at thickest part of breast is 165 degrees for game hens, 180 degrees for partridge, and juices run clear. Remove from oven.

WHILE THE BIRDS ARE ROASTING, MAKE THE FIG SAUCE:

- Place olive oil in the same pan as bacon cooked in, over low-medium heat. Add shallots and cook about 5 minutes or until softened and just starting to turn color to golden brown, scraping to release any bacon bits. Add garlic and cook for about 2 minutes, being careful not to brown the garlic.
- Add all remaining ingredients to pan: figs, bacon, orange juice, red wine, vinegar, honey, bay leaf, and thyme. Season with a pinch of pepper. Cover the pan and cook for 20 minutes on medium heat, stirring occasionally. Remove from heat.
- Strain the sauce through a sieve placed over a heatproof bowl or container. Remove the bacon slices, bay leaf, and thyme from sieve; discard. Leave figs in sieve. Use the back of a spoon to press the figs firmly to force through sieve. When the figs have been completely pressed, scrape bottom of sieve into your bowl. Discard contents of sieve. Return sauce back into pan and heat before serving.
- If the sauce is too thin, return to medium heat until desired consistency. If sauce is too thick, add a splash of red wine. Season to taste with salt and pepper.
- Place birds on serving dish. Brush or spoon fig sauce over birds. Serve.

Prayers

TRADITIONAL PRAYER

Let nothing disturb you.
Let nothing make you afraid.
All things are passing.
God alone never changes.
Patience gains all things.
If you have God you will want for nothing.
God alone suffices.

CONTEMPORARY PRAYER

St. Teresa, help me to distinguish between times of penance and times of partridge in my life and to act accordingly. Amen.

CHAPTER 3

St. Brigit of Ireland

rigit and Teresa walked side-by-side into the room. They couldn't have made for a more unlikely pair—Teresa with her dance shoes, brightly colored dress, and flashing dark eyes looked every bit the high-spirited Spaniard she was. On the other hand, Brigit in her gray-brown cloak and sturdy shoes looked demure, while the bright red hair cascading wildly over her shoulders gave more than a hint of her fiery nature. Their former guardian angels often said that it was a good thing that the two didn't live at the same time or the angels would have asked for new assignments.

"I think that's where we put the food," Teresa said. "It looks like it's organized according to dishes." She pointed to elegant calligraphic labels indicating "appetizers," "main dishes," "vegetables," "desserts," and other categories. "I'll bet my dance shoes that Martha is behind this." Brigit gave a snort-laugh in agreement. "I've brought a main dish, so I guess I'd better put it where it belongs," Teresa said, moving toward the middle of the table.

Brigit studied the long line of food, then spotted a smaller table off to one side. It was loaded with every variety of bread you could imagine. She nodded approvingly. *There has to be bread,* she thought. *Bread is the staff of life, even up here.* She moved to the table, pushed several loaves to the back, unwrapped a block of pale yellow butter and a jar of sloe jam she had been carrying in the folds of her cloak, and placed them next to the bread. *Can't have bread without butter. Or jam,* she thought.

More than ten percent of the Irish have ginger or red hair—the highest percentage of any population. We don't know what color hair Brigit had, but red is a possibility.

· · · · · · · · · · · · · · · · · ·

Butter is associated with Brigit because it is believed she often gave butter and other dairy goods to the poor. Sloes, a sour, blackberry-like fruit from the blackthorn tree, have been a popular food for millennia. The 5,300-year-old mummy called Otzi who was discovered in the Austrian Alps had eaten sloes as part of his last meal.

She then reached deeper in her cloak, which seemed to have endless folds, and removed a pottery jug with a cloth stopper. The nose-tingling smell of freshly brewed beer made her smile. It was a particularly flavorful batch, with a hardy, earthy tang, just the way she liked it.

In Brigit's time, beer was not the potent alcoholic beverage it is today. It had an alcohol content of about two percent compared to five percent or more today. Beer was consumed daily by all social classes, but the idea that it was drunk in place of water is a myth. However, the boiling and fermentation process did kill off some of the harmful bacteria in water, so people tended to drink beer more freely and at younger ages than we do today.

"Is there a place to put some beer?" she asked Solanus Casey, as he shuffled past her to answer the door. He didn't seem to hear her, and a brief hint of what might have been impatience in her earthly life clouded her blue eyes. "Excuse me," she said a little louder. "Where should I put the beer?"

"Oh." Solanus blinked. "Over there, I think." He gestured toward the back of the room, where large stone jars filled with wine were standing.

Brigit balanced her pottery jug on the lid of one of the stone jars. *I'd take a swig now, but I'd better wait for the party,* she thought. Looking at the long table set for the guests, she said aloud to no one in particular, "Good thing the 'Cana Clause' applies to beer as well as wine or I'd have had to bring an entire wagon of beer!"

Fumbling once again in the folds of her cloak, she brought out a pan of what looked like black bread. Locating the area for desserts, she nearly bumped into John the Baptist, who was heading in the same direction. She set her pan down next to a comb dripping with golden honey. "So what did you bring?" she asked him. "Carob-covered grasshoppers again?"

John frowned slightly. "No," he said a bit gruffly. "Last time I brought them I had to take the whole plate home. I was eating bugs for days." He brightened a bit. "So this time I brought lightly salted roasted locusts for an appetizer. They are very crunchy," he added enthusiastically.

"That sounds . . . interesting," Brigit said, then wrinkled her brow at the plate of little ball-like bites he had just placed on the table. "But this isn't the area for appetizers." She pointed to the "Dessert" sign. "And that doesn't look like locusts to me. It looks more like . . . dates."

John dropped his eyes. "I was getting tired of people not wanting to try my food, so this time I brought some carob honey dates, as well as locusts. I keep trying to encourage people to eat healthy, but they just laugh and say that we can finally eat all the dessert we want. The locusts are up there," he added, gesturing toward the start of the food line.

Brigit laughed a deep, hearty laugh that even made John smile a bit. "Eat dessert first," she said, then leaning closer, added, "We can be partners in crime, er . . . virtue." She pointed to her own plate. "I brought my usual butter and jam and beer, but I also brought chocolate brownies made with Guinness!" She pulled the cover off, letting the heady aroma of chocolate fill the air.

John shook his head in disapproval. "You didn't eat chocolate. You never even heard of chocolate," he said. "And there wasn't anything like Guinness in your time. Now, let's have my carob and dates. At least they are historically correct!"

"I know you've never tasted Guinness, but have you ever eaten chocolate?" Brigit demanded.

"No," said John.

"Here." Brigit broke off a piece of the brownie and handed it to him. "Just try it."

John nibbled the edge and nodded somewhat approvingly. "Not bad."

"Not bad? I'd say it was heavenly!" Brigit chuckled. "Much better than locusts, wouldn't you agree?"

The earliest traces of chocolate have been found in pottery used by the Olmec people who lived in what is now Mexico around 1,000 BC. Most Meso-Americans, including the Maya and Aztecs, consumed chocolate. The Spanish explorer Hernan Cortes may have been the first European to encounter it in the form of a frothy drink. By the 1600s, chocolate was popular in Europe, although sugar, honey, vanilla, and even pepper were added to make it less bitter.

"I did quite well living on locusts," John replied. But Brigit watched as John broke off another piece of brownie and headed to the far side of the room where Francis Borgia was leaning against the fireplace mantle, deep in conversation with Augustine. She made sure her brownies weren't hidden behind the carob bites before walking around the long ivory table. Each side had eight nameplates written in silver letters. She found hers on the right side, between Kateri Tekawitha and Francis of Assisi. She glanced toward the head of the table where an especially ornate card was displayed. *Well, we know who will be sitting there,* she thought. She was debating whether she dared slip back to the wine jar bar and pour herself a glass of beer when a squeaking noise made her startle. A diminutive man with a square face, wide-set eyes, and a thin grin was standing behind her. "Martin! You startled me." Cradled in the palm of his hand was a gray mouse. Brigit suddenly noticed the animal and frowned. "You brought Squeaky?"

Martin de Porres nodded. "He wanted to come. He won't be any bother."

Brigit shook her head. "You know that some people . . . Martha," she whispered under her breath, "aren't going to be thrilled with a mouse in the house."

He nodded again and slipped the furry rodent deep into the sleeve of his habit. "Mum's the word," he whispered.

Brigit smiled. No one could be upset with Martin. He radiated love and kindness to all creatures—even mice. "Well, Francesco won't mind," she said. "Patron of animals and all that. What did you bring for the feast?" She changed the topic before someone else spotted the mouse.

"Oh, something vegetarian," Martin said. "But I'm sure you'll love it. And you? Beer, butter, and jam, I presume."

"Of course," Brigit said. "And a surprise dish, too."

"A surprise for our honored guests!"

They both looked toward the place card at the head of the table and nodded.

Did You Know?

Brigit means "high" or "exalted."

St. Brigit of Ireland

453 – 525

Legends and myths surround the life of St. Brigit of Ireland or Brigit of Kildare, not the least of which is how she spelled her name. To distinguish her from St. Bridget of Sweden, Brigit is the more common spelling, although she is sometimes fondly called Bride. The controversy begins with her very existence. We aren't even completely positive that she was a real person since she has the same name and general attributes as the Celtic goddess Brigit. Like St. Brigit, the goddess Brigit was associated with spring, fertility, poetry, and healing. Not to mention that St. Brigit's feast day was originally celebrated on the same day as the pagan festival of Imbolc that heralded the beginning of spring. However, it is also plausible and even probable that her mother named her daughter a traditional Irish name prior to her conversion to Christianity, and then that daughter grew up to become a saint.

Because of numerous legends about Brigit, it's hard to sort fact from fiction, but it's generally thought she was born in County Louth, Ireland, in 451. Her father is said to be Dubhthach, a Leinster chieftain, and her mother is believed to have been Brocca, Dubhthach's Pict slave and mistress, who had been converted to Christianity by St. Patrick. Dubhthach's wife was less than thrilled that her husband had a child with Brocca, so she had both Brocca and Brigit sold to a druid. It is claimed that Brigit couldn't eat anything the pagan druid fed her, so she was miraculously fed by a white cow with red ears. (The importance of the red ears is unknown.)

The story goes that when she was about ten, Brigit was returned to her father's house, where she promptly began giving away his possessions to the poor, including the butter and cheese from his cows! Once again, Dubhthach (one might speculate that it was actually Dubhthach's wife) tried to sell Brigit into slavery, but the king who was to buy her recognized her holiness and convinced Dubhthach to free her.

Around 480, Brigit and seven companions founded a double monastery at Kildare on the site of a shrine to the goddess Brigit. (Things might have been a bit less confusing for history if she had selected a site dedicated to a different goddess.) Not uncommon for the day, a double monastery was an area of communal living with separate spaces for men and women. The monastery at Kildare was governed for centuries by abbot-bishops for the men and abbesses for the women, with the Abbess of Kildare being given special accord.

Brigit was known for performing many miracles, most of which involved healing the sick and feeding the poor. She also is said to have founded an art school specializing in illuminated manuscripts.

The Book of Kells, the most famous illuminated manuscript from the British Isles, was created around AD 800, more than 300 years after Brigit.

Tradition says that she remained friends with St. Patrick throughout her life, with the ninth-century Canon of Patrick claiming, "Between St. Patrick and St. Brigid, the pillars of the Irish people, there was so great a friendship of charity that they had but one heart and one mind. Through him and through her Christ performed many great works."

Brigit's close friend and student Darlugdach was at her side when she died on February 1, 525. Because she lived before there was a formal canonization process for saints, she was simply acclaimed one and has remained so ever since. She has more than twenty patronages including cattle, dairy workers, fugitives, and children whose parents aren't married.

Legends, Lore, and Miracles

Legend has it that one time Brigit was given a gift of apples and sweet sloes. A group of lepers begged her for the apples, so she gave them away. Apparently, she kept the sweet sloes, also called blackthorns, which are a small, bluish-purple fruit somewhat like sour plums used to make various kinds of liquors, including Sloe Gin.

A variation on this legend says that the woman who gave her the apples and sweet sloes was angry that Brigid gave them away. Brigid herself got so angry at the woman for her selfishness that she cursed the woman's tree, and it never bore fruit again. (Curses are popular with Irish saints.) She was also said to have been able to turn water into beer.

Once a leper refused to let her heal him, saying he got more help being sick than he would get if he were well. Brigit healed him anyway.

Brigit is said to have converted the King of Leinster to Christianity and convinced him to give her the land on which to build a convent. The land contained many berry bushes, and the convent became famous for making jam. As the story goes, she asked the king for as much land as her cloak would cover. When the king agreed, she had four of her sisters each take a corner and run as far as they could until the cloak covered many acres. The king was dismayed but gave her the choice plot she wanted along with the promise of continued support.

Quote
"I should like a great lake of beer for the King of Kings. I should like the angels of Heaven to be drinking it through time eternal.**"**

Recipe

Brownies with Guinness Fudge Sauce

This brownie creates its own rich fudge sauce while cooking. As a tribute to Brigit, the recipe uses Kerrygold Butter and a nice strong stout or dark beer, such as Guinness Stout. The rich, dark flavors of cocoa, stout, and coffee combine for a decadent dessert. Wonderful served warm out of the oven with ice cream.

- **PREP TIME:** 20 minutes
- **COOK TIME:** 40 minutes
- **SERVES:** 6-8
- **SPECIAL EQUIPMENT NEEDED:** 8" or 9" baking pan (square or round) or a 2-quart baking dish
- **THIS RECIPE CAN BE LACTO-OVO VEGETARIAN,** if you don't serve with ice cream.
- **MAKE IT GLUTEN-FREE,** but note that the consistency and outcome may vary by using gluten-free flour. Use a gluten-free flour blend, such as King Arthur Measure-To-Measure, or Bob's Red Mill 1-To-1. Make sure the following ingredients are labeled as gluten-free: stout or dark beer, coffee powder, vanilla extract, baking powder, and baking soda. And as always, ensure that all the ingredients you use do not contain gluten.

INGREDIENTS

6 tablespoons or 3 ounces unsalted butter*

1 cup sugar, divided

½ cup brown sugar, plus 1/3 cup brown sugar, separate

½ cup unsweetened cocoa powder, divided

1 cup flour

1½ teaspoons baking powder

1 teaspoon baking soda

½ cup whole milk, room temperature

2 teaspoons vanilla extract, divided

¼ teaspoon salt, plus a pinch, divided

¾ cup strong brewed coffee (or ¾ cup very hot water mixed with 1½ tablespoons instant coffee)

¾ cup Guinness Stout or similar dark beer or stout

*If using salted butter, reduce salt in brownie batter to ⅛ teaspoon

DIRECTIONS

- Preheat oven to 350 degrees Fahrenheit with oven rack placed in center of oven.
- Grease a 9" x 9" baking pan, or equivalent size baking pan or casserole dish.
- Melt butter in a medium saucepan. Remove from heat.
- Place in a small bowl: flour, baking powder, baking soda and ¼ teaspoon salt. Stir to combine.
- Add to pot that contains melted butter: ½ cup sugar, ½ cup packed brown sugar, and ¼ cup cocoa. Stir well. Slowly stir in milk and 1 teaspoon vanilla. Then stir in your flour / baking powder / baking soda / salt mixture. Beat by hand until just smooth; do not overmix.
- Scrape batter into prepared baking pan.
- In a small bowl, combine ⅓ cup brown sugar, ½ cup sugar, ¼ cup cocoa powder, and a pinch of salt. Sprinkle this mixture over the batter; do not mix in.
- Heat in small pan on stovetop until very hot but not boiling (or heat in microwave using microwave-safe container): ¾ cup strong coffee (or ¾ cup water with 1½ tablespoons instant coffee mixed in) and ¾ cup Guinness Stout or dark beer/stout. Add 1 teaspoon vanilla extract. Pour this over the batter that has been sprinkled with sugar mixture. Do not stir.
- Bake for 40 minutes. Let stand for 10 minutes. Serve by scooping out some brownie onto a plate, then spooning some of the Guinness Fudge Sauce over it. (The sauce is created underneath the brownie while it bakes.) Wonderful with ice cream or whipped cream.

Prayers

TRADITIONAL PRAYER

I would like the angels of Heaven to be among us.

I would like an abundance of peace.

I would like full vessels of charity.

I would like rich treasures of mercy.

I would like cheerfulness to preside over all.

I would like Jesus to be present.

I would like the three Marys of illustrious renown to be with us.

I would like the friends of Heaven to be gathered around us from all parts.

I would like myself to be a rent payer to the Lord; that I should suffer distress, that he would bestow a good blessing upon me.

I would like a great lake of beer for the King of Kings.

I would like to be watching Heaven's family drinking it through all eternity

CONTEMPORARY PRAYER

St. Brigit, help me to overcome any struggles of my childhood or my past to become the person of God I was created to be. Amen.

CHAPTER 4

St. John the Baptist

John the Baptist stopped short when he saw that Francis Borgia was deep into a heated discussion with Augustine. At first, he thought they might have been discussing theology, but then he realized they were talking about the relative merits of American football versus soccer. He turned around when he heard Augustine say, "There has to be a reason they are called the Saints!" Since he had no knowledge of either sport, and even less desire to gain any knowledge, he moseyed back toward the buffet table. His locust appetizer appeared untouched, so he scooped up a handful and began munching. They were quite tasty, but the little antennae tended to get stuck in one's teeth.

He could use something to wash them down, but the jars that once held water were now brimming with wine, and even in heaven, John was abstentious. There would be water once the dinner got started. He told himself he could wait until then.

He hadn't attended many dinner parties in heaven—one or two in honor of the Virgin, at which his mother, Elizabeth, had insisted he make an appearance, and a couple of the almost mandatory Easter gatherings. *Everyone talks about how Jesus's mom had been pushy at that wedding in Cana*, he thought. *They clearly have never met my mom!* The family joke was that John lived in the desert because that was the one place his mother couldn't nag him to get a real job.

John probably did eat actual locusts since they are a good source of protein and would be easy to prepare over an open fire (or eaten raw). However, since locusts tend to live in well-watered areas—not deserts where John wandered—and are somewhat seasonal, he probably also ate the pods of the locust or carob tree. In fact, the tree is sometimes called Saint John's Bread. In any event, his diet was very limited.

Although John and Jesus are often called "cousins" in popular lore, they probably weren't cousins in the sense we use the term. For one thing, although the Scriptures say that Mary had a sister—"Now there stood by the cross of Jesus his mother, and his mother's sister, Mary of Clopas, and Mary Magdalene"—Elizabeth is never mentioned as Mary's sister. Instead, she and Mary were said to be "kinswomen," a more distant relationship, perhaps, as some have suggested, what we would call second cousins, which would make John and Jesus something like third cousins. The other options that would allow John and Jesus to be first cousins would entail Joseph and Zechariah being brothers, Elizabeth being Joseph's sister, or Zechariah being Mary's brother, none of which have ever been considered as possibilities.

• • • • • • • • • • • • • • • • • • •

The disputed area known today as the West Bank takes its name from the west bank of the Jordan River.

John found dinner parties a wee bit uncomfortable. The only one he had "attended" when he was on earth was Herod's birthday party, and that didn't end quite the way he would have liked it. When Peter invited him to this event, John had paused long enough for Peter to ask if there was a problem. "There won't be, um, platters, will there?" John asked. He thought about one ill-timed, secret visit to earth when he had happened to drop by a Tudor feast where a pig's head was served on a platter. The thought still gave him shudders. Peter assured him that there wouldn't be any platters, with pigs' heads or otherwise, and John reluctantly agreed to attend.

He would much rather have paid a quick visit. People on earth didn't realize just how often the saints check out their old stomping grounds. John especially liked to keep track of what was going on in the Middle East even though, after more than 2,000 years, things hadn't changed much either in terms of the landscape or the politics. John wasn't interested in the politics anymore ("Above my pay grade these days," he liked to say), but sometimes he craved the desert. Heaven was lovely, of course, but there was nothing like barren, rocky landscapes to refresh the spirit. He had visited other deserts, like those in the Americas and Australia, but there was nothing like that slip of land along the Jordan River as far as he was concerned.

John had more free time to visit earth than some of the other saints. He felt fortunate that he wasn't called on constantly for favors, like Anthony who was always finding lost keys or Jude who had to deal with impossible cases day in and day out. He was happy to deal with the occasional prayer or novena that was sent his way but was glad that most of the time he was relegated to Bible stories.

He brushed a bit of salty locust from his camel hair jacket. He supposed it was understandable, but most new arrivals in heaven expected him to wear a shaggy, one-shouldered garment instead of the sleek jacket he generally sported. "Those Renaissance artists are to blame," he once complained to his former disciple, Andrew. "They just assumed that I wore a not very well tanned camel hide. Can you imagine how impractical that would have been when I was baptizing people? Those artists obviously never smelled wet camel hair. Not to mention going around half-naked would have been stupid. They never spent a night in the desert, much less in a wet camel hide. And why would I would want to spend eternity wearing something that itchy, smelly, and uncomfortable?"

John decided to find his name tag on the table to kill a little time. He was pleased to be seated next to Andrew Kim. He didn't know much about Korea, but he did know that silk moth pupae were a common snack food. He and Kim could discuss the protein value of insects if nothing else.

It is possible that John wore an actual camel's hide, but it is more likely that he wore a rough-woven cloak made from camel's hair. The wooly hair of camels can be pulled out in tufts that can be used for tents and clothing. Camel hair is an ideal material for use in the desert since, like wool, it is both sun-protective and insulating. Today camel hair garments are usually named for their color and style, not their fabric, which may or may not contain actual camel hair.

• • • • • • • • • • • • • • • • • • • •

In Asia, the tradition of eating insects dates back at least 3,000 years. Roast silk moth pupae are commonly eaten in China, Japan, Vietnam, and Thailand, as well as Korea.

The room was beginning to fill with guests. John sighed and then made a decision. He walked over to the buffet table, picked up his bowl of salted locusts, and joined Teresa of Avila and Gertrude of Nivelles, who were chatting together in a corner. "Anyone care to try some roasted locusts?" he asked. No one took him up on the offer.

Did You Know?

In some countries, the summer solstice is dedicated to St. John because it occurs on or near his major feast day.

St. John the Baptist

UNKNOWN – ABOUT AD 33

J
ohn was born somewhere in Judea in the late first century BC. His father, Zechariah, was a Jewish priest, and his mother, Elizabeth, was a kinswoman of the Virgin Mary. The Gospel of Luke says that the angel Gabriel, who apparently was quite busy with birth announcements at the time, told Zechariah he would become a father even though Elizabeth was too old to bear children. Like most everyone who sees an angel, Zechariah was "gripped with fear." Gabriel went on to say that this son would be "great in the sight of the Lord," adding that he would never drink anything alcoholic. (These two prophecies are probably not interrelated.) Finally, Gabriel said that the child would make the people ready for the Lord.

Zechariah was doubtful, so Gabriel said that because of his disbelief, Zechariah would be unable to speak until "the appointed time." Zechariah was doing his priestly duties at the temple when all this happened. After he returned home, Elizabeth became pregnant. (We don't know how Zechariah explained to her his inability to speak or how he explained why she became pregnant after all the years of infertility.) We then hear of John leaping for joy in his mother's womb when Mary came to visit, but we know nothing of his childhood or youth.

He suddenly appears as a full-fledged prophet preaching his message of repentance to people in the lower Jordan Valley. Some scholars think that he may have belonged to the Essenes, a strict Judaic sect that anticipated the arrival of the Messiah and practiced ritual washing (*mikveh*, in Judaism), which for Christians became baptism. It is certain that John did use immersion in the river as a sign of repentance, and he even baptized Jesus himself in the Jordan River.

It is generally believed that John baptized Jesus at the site of Al-Maghtas on the Jordanian side of the Jordan River. Pilgrims come to both the Israeli and the Jordanian sides of the river on pilgrimage. In John's time, the Jordan River was much larger and wilder. The flow rate was four times greater then, than it is today.

John died, not as a direct result of his Messianic preaching or recognition of Jesus, but because Herod had him killed, either as a gift to his stepdaughter, as Christian tradition has long taught, or as a rebellious force. This despite the fact Herod believed John was a good man.

Although most of our information about John comes from the Gospels, he is one of the rare biblical figures who has been noted in a secular history of the time. Flavius Josephus, the Roman historian, in his *Antiquities of the Jews,* written in about AD 93, says that John was "a good man" who commanded the Jews to "exercise virtue towards one another, and pity towards God, and so to come to baptism." In the Gospel of Matthew, John was put to death because he was overtly critical of the marriage of Herod to Herodias, the ex-wife of his brother Philip. It is said that after enjoying his stepdaughter Salome's dance, Herod offered her anything she wanted. With the encouragement of her mother, Salome asked for John's head on a platter, and Herod reluctantly agreed. In Josephus's account, Herod had John put to death "to prevent any mischief he might cause." The nature of John's death is not detailed, but Josephus says that it occurred at Herod's hilltop palace at Macherus.

John is remembered by Catholics on June 24, his birthday, and on August 29, the commemoration of his beheading. The Orthodox Church has four additional feasts in his honor, including his conception on September 22 and the First and Second Finding of the Head of Saint John the Forerunner on February 24. He is the patron saint of Jordan, Puerto Rico, and French Canada, among others.

Legends, Lore, and Miracles

John's burial place is unknown, although it is said to have been at what is now the site of Saint John the Baptist mosque in what is currently Palestinian territory.

The Umayyad Mosque in Damascus, Syria, is the official site of the final resting place of the head of the Baptist. Pope John Paul II visited the shrine in 2001. However, the head was also said to be in Rome, Amiens, Antioch, and even Kent in England. His right hand is supposed to be in Istanbul but also on Mount Athos. His left hand is alleged to be in an Armenian church.

DNA tests on bones in a Bulgarian church that were long believed to have been those of John indicate they came from a Middle Eastern man who lived about the time of John, although there is no concrete evidence that they are actually the bones of the Baptist.

John is considered a prophet in Islam, and the story of his conception is even told in the Qur'an.

Quote

"Repent, for the Kingdom of Heaven is at hand!"
(Matt. 3:2)

Recipe

————————◆◆◆————————

Carob-Almond Date Bites with Honey

This recipe utilizes ingredients that would have been available in the days of John the Baptist, as well as giving homage to the "locust" or carob that he probably ate. It's a lovely treat to serve guests or share as gifts for the holidays.

- **PREP TIME:** 10-15 minutes
- **COOK TIME:** 20 minutes
- **YIELD:** 20 individual bites
- **MAKE IT VEGAN** by substituting agave syrup for honey.

This recipe is gluten-free but, as always, check your ingredients for gluten content.

INGREDIENTS

8 oz. pitted dates

⅔ cup water

½ cup almonds, ground fine using a food processor or blender or ½ cup almond flour (Optional: additional ¼ cup for rolling)

½ cup carob powder (roasted carob powder), plus additional ¼ cup for coating

¼ cup honey

⅛ teaspoon sea salt, or a healthy pinch

DIRECTIONS

- Put dates and water in a small saucepan. Mix and cook over medium heat for 20 minutes, stirring occasionally. Watch that water doesn't evaporate – add ¼ cup additional water at a time if this happens.
- Place almond flour (or ground almonds) in a dry sauté / frying pan over medium-high heat. Stir often until the almond flour is toasted / golden; it can burn quickly. Transfer to a dish to cool.
- Place dates in a medium bowl and mash with a fork until smooth. (You may alternately use a food processor with steel blade: pulse until smooth). Add the toasted almond flour, carob flour, honey, and sea salt. Mix well until ingredients are thoroughly combined.

- Taste and adjust for flavor and texture. If too thin, add a bit more carob powder. If too thick, add a few drops water.
- Put additional ¼ cup carob powder into a small bowl with high sides, such as a cereal bowl. If also rolling in ground almonds, have a separate bowl with some ground almonds or almond flour.
- Scoop a teaspoon of the date/carob mixture into your hands and roll into a ball. Roll each ball in carob powder and/or ground almonds.
- You may serve immediately, or place in airtight container, refrigerated, for up to a week. You may also freeze them by placing on a metal pan and placing in freezer for a few hours. Once they are frozen, place them in a freezer bag, push out any air to avoid freezer burn, and freeze for up to 6 months.

Prayers

TRADITIONAL PRAYER

O glorious Saint John the Baptist, greatest prophet among those born of woman, although thou wast sanctified in thy mother's womb and didst lead a most innocent life, nevertheless it was thy will to retire into the wilderness, there to devote thyself to the practice of austerity and penance; obtain for us of thy Lord the grace to be wholly detached, at least in our hearts, from earthly goods, and to practice Christian mortification with interior recollection and with the spirit of holy prayer.

CONTEMPORARY PRAYER

S aint John, be with me as I cross the deserts of my life. Help me to find the honey-like sweetness that exists even in the hardest of times and give me the ability to recognize my sins and repent. Amen.

CHAPTER 5

St. Martin de Porres

Martin de Porres joined Brigit, who was standing near the wine jars. "It's beginning to fill up," he said. Brigit nodded. "Do you know what time the honored guest will arrive?" he asked.

"Soon, I would think," Brigid said, "but then a thousand days are like one day here, and one day is like a thousand, so who knows."

"True," Martin nodded. He was never one to rush—unless there was a very good reason—and there was almost never a very good reason.

"Martha said she would make my dish for me," Martin said. "She says she is a much better cook than I am. I didn't disagree," he said with a twinkle in his eye. "If she wants to stand over the stove she can. I spent enough time in the kitchen when I was in the monastery."

"What is Martha making?" Brigit asked him.

"Quinoa and lima bean patties," Martin said. "Simple food, but very filling. Speaking of which, I had better go see if she needs any help. She wants people to offer to help, but I think that's because she likes telling them that she can handle it better on her own. Don't tell her I said that," he added conspiratorially.

"Wouldn't think of it. Better not let her see Squeaky or you'll both be chased out with her broom," Brigid added.

Martin nodded and felt his sleeve, making sure that the mouse was well hidden. "We'll be careful."

Principal crops grown in Peru, Martin's birthplace, include quinoa, lima beans, sweet potatoes, and potatoes. In addition, squash, peanuts, and cotton date back at least 10,000 years or more. Peru still provides half the world's quinoa.

• • • • • • • • • • • • • • • • • • •

Among his many gifts, Martin had an extraordinary ability to communicate, seemingly telepathically, with animals. This ability is the source of many of the legends about him.

He headed toward the back of the cottage, where Martha's kitchen was located. Before he reached the open arch leading to a room with several ovens and a huge stovetop, a soft mewling sound made him pause. He glanced around, but not seeing anything, stood on tiptoe, and peered over the windowsill. He looked down at a pair of golden eyes staring back at him through thick leaves. "Oh, you dear thing," he said. "Wait right there."

He rushed into the kitchen. "Where are you off to?" Martha asked, a spatula in her hand and a griddle filled with pancake-like patties on the stove. "Your quinoa patties are nearly done."

"Be right back," Martin said, pushing open the back door and running into the garden. He cocked his head to one side until he heard the faint meow again. Following the sound, he located a large gray cat in the middle of a holly bush. "How did you get there?" he asked, gently pulling the furry bundle out into the open. The cat, immediately recognizing Martin as an animal lover, began purring loudly. "Now what am I going to do with you?" Martin asked, and the cat purred even more loudly. He pulled her onto his lap and began petting her. "You're a big one, aren't you?" he said. The cat, a Maine Coon, shivered as Martin wrapped it into his robes. "You don't belong here," he said. "You belong over at the Rainbow Bridge, I'll bet." Some people still didn't believe in the Rainbow Bridge, Martin thought. But it was real. Very real.

Looking around to see if anyone was watching, Martin closed his eyes and willed himself across heaven. Even though transporting was perfectly acceptable here, Martin remembered the disapproval he experienced when he did this on earth. He only transported under the most serious of situations— and an out-of-place cat qualified as a serious situation.

Martin suddenly appeared in the middle of a grassy meadow. All around him, dogs and cats and horses and birds and every kind of animal that had ever deeply loved a human and been deeply loved in return were playing in the sunshine. The archangel Raphael, who spent any time when he wasn't being called on as a healer at the Rainbow Bridge, greeted Martin. "Who do you have?" he asked.

The idea of the Rainbow Bridge is derived from a poem of the same name:

Just this side of heaven is a place called Rainbow Bridge.

When an animal dies that has been especially close to someone here, that pet goes to Rainbow Bridge. There are meadows and hills for all of our special friends so they can run and play together. There is plenty of food, water, and sunshine, and our friends are warm and comfortable.

All the animals who had been ill and old are restored to health and vigor. Those who were hurt or maimed are made whole and strong again, just as we remember them in our dreams of days and times gone by. The animals are happy and content, except for one small thing; they each miss someone very special to them, who had to be left behind.

They all run and play together, but the day comes when one suddenly stops and looks into the distance. His bright eyes are intent. His eager body quivers. Suddenly he begins to run from the group, flying over the green grass, his legs carrying him faster and faster.

You have been spotted, and when you and your special friend finally meet, you cling together in joyous reunion, never to be parted again. The happy kisses rain upon your face; your hands again caress the beloved head, and you look once more into the trusting eyes of your pet, so long gone from your life but never absent from your heart.

Then you cross Rainbow Bridge together . . .

Author unknown

Martin touched his head to the cat's forehead and listened intently as the cat appeared to talk to him. "Mittens," he said. "He wants to know if his person is here."

Raphael shook his head. "Not that I know." He reached over and took Mittens in his arms. "We'll keep Mittens safe. Tell him that he will know when his person arrives. They always do."

Raphael is one of the patrons of healing, but in the book of Tobit, he accompanies Tobias and his dog. This is a notable mention in the Bible of a domesticated or pet animal.

Martin nodded and started to close his eyes in preparation for his return to the party. All of a sudden, he heard Mittens cry out, and he saw the cat spring from Raphael's arms. There, at the far end of the meadow, a man was sprinting toward them. Mittens bounded across the field and leaped into the man's arms, nearly knocking him to the ground.

"Oh Mittens, you made it," the man cried as tears of joy ran down his face. "You made it." Mittens purred and laid a paw on the man's cheek. "It wouldn't have been heaven without you." The man began to sob, deep heart-rending sobs of joy. "I just knew you'd be here," he said over and over. "I am so glad to see you." Mittens bumped his head against his person's chin with an excited meow.

Raphael and Martin exchanged a knowing look. "I'd better get back to the party," Martin said finally. He looked one last time at the man, who was sitting cross-legged in the grass, cradling Mittens, who was kneading his chest. With a jolt, Martin returned to the garden outside Martha's kitchen, but even at this distance, he swore he could still hear Mittens purring.

Did You Know?

St. Rose of Lima and St. Martin were close friends.

St. Martin de Porres
DECEMBER 9, 1579 – NOVEMBER 3, 1639

J uan Martin de Porres Velázquez was born in Lima, Peru, the son of a Spanish nobleman and his African-Native American mistress.

After his sister was born two years later, his father, apparently dismayed that his children resembled their dark-skinned mother too much, abandoned the family, and Martin's mother took in laundry to support herself and her children. When Martin was twelve, his mother apprenticed him with a barber-surgeon, where, in addition to learning how to cut hair, he also learned some basic medical practices, including caring for wounds and administering medications.

Martin worked as a barber-surgeon, but his heart was always directed toward God. His faith and devotion grew, and he longed to enter religious life, but under Peruvian law, people of color could not become full members of religious orders. Finally, when he was about fifteen, he asked the Dominicans of Holy Rosary Priory in Lima if he could become a *donado*, a "lay helper" who performed servant duties in exchange for living in the community.

At the time, barbers also doubled as medical professionals. In addition to cutting hair, they could draw blood (a common practice said to eliminate disease), pull teeth, prepare ointments and some medications. This combination, which seems odd to modern thinking, continued until the mid-eighteenth century. The red and white pole that used to stand outside barbershops indicated the blood and cloths used during surgical procedures, especially bloodletting.

• •

Dominicans were among the first missionaries to the Americans. They established a house in the modern-day Dominican Republic in 1509. The Peruvian province was established in 1540. In February 2020, the Dominican province in Peru converted its formation house in Lima into the Hospital of the Charity of St. Martin de Porres, citing for the change the example of Martin of using as an infirmary the monastery where he lived.

His training as a barber afforded him some additional value to the monastery. Since friars were required to wear the tonsure, the traditional haircut with a bald spot on top, each religious community had to have its own barber. He also did the most menial of tasks such as laundry, cleaning, and kitchen duty. He never asked to be more than a *donado*, but after eight years, the prior allowed him to take vows as a member of the Third Order of Saint Dominic. Some suggested that this might have come about due to his father's intercession, but his religious devotion was never in question. Unfortunately, prejudice was present even in the monastery, with one novice calling Martin a "mulatto dog" and a priest mocking him for being illegitimate. About ten years after taking his vows, he was assigned to the infirmary, where he put his skills as a medical professional to good use. Nevertheless, Martin was always keenly aware of his social status as a person of color and the dislike of some of his fellows. Once, when the monastery was in debt, he said, "I am only a poor mulatto, sell me. I am the property of the order. Sell me."

His medical training combined with what seemed to be a supernatural ability to cure the sick, and this brought him recognition. His patients included the rich as well as the poor, but he treated everyone the same, from Spanish nobles to slaves recently brought to the Americas. Once, to the horror of his fellow Dominicans, he brought a dying beggar to his own bed. When criticized, he simply said, "Compassion is preferable to cleanliness."

One of Martin's primary duties was to beg for alms. It is said that he was able to feed more than 150 poor people every day from what he collected as well as provide substantial funds for charity. One of his lesser-known charitable activities was to provide the necessary dowry of 4,000 pesos to enable at least twenty-seven poor women to marry. Another notable achievement was the foundation of the Orphanage and School of the Holy Cross, where young orphans were taught trades and homemaking skills. In addition, he convinced his sister, with whom he was always close, to open a hospice on her property in the country and, as if that weren't enough, he also brought stray and injured animals to her, thus creating the first veterinary/ humane society where he applied his healing abilities to animals as well.

Martin died of a fever when he was fifty-nine, surrounded by his fellow Dominicans. His last words were said to be "*et homo factus est*" ("Christ was made man") from the Creed. He was canonized in 1962 by Pope John XXIII and is buried at the Convento Santo Domingo in Lima.

Martin is the patron of people of color, barbers, hairdressers, race relations, social justice, public health, and public education, among others. His feast day is November 3. He is often shown with a dog, a cat, a bird, and a mouse eating from the same bowl at his feet.

Legends, Lore, and Miracles

It was said that some of his fellow friars would hide the potholders when Martin worked in the kitchen. He would lift the scalding pots from the fire with his bare hands, but he would never get burned.

When he prayed, the room was filled with a mysterious light, and he was seen to levitate when in a state of religious ecstasy. He was also seen to be kneeling a foot or more above the ground when he was in one of his many all-night vigils.

After his death, so many people took a piece of his habit as a relic, it is said that he had to be redressed three times.

Other friars claimed that Martin often passed through locked doors to care for the sick who had been isolated. Although he never physically left Lima, he is said to have been seen as far away as Africa, China, and Japan. One story says that a man who was being shipped to the Americas to be a slave was consoled by Martin. He eventually saw Martin in Peru and asked when he had come there, only to learn that Martin had never left Lima. He is also said to have been able to cure the sick simply by offering them a glass of water.

One story goes that mice had nested in the monasteries' collection of fine linens (presumably for Mass vestments.) The friars wanted to poison them, but Martin caught one of the mice and said, "Little brothers, why are you and your companions doing so much harm to the things belonging to the sick? Look, I won't kill you, but you should assemble all your friends and lead them to the far end of the garden. Every day I will bring you food if you leave the wardrobe alone." The mice promptly followed Martin to the garden and never bothered the linen again.

Quote

"Everything, even sweeping, scraping vegetables, weeding a garden, and waiting on the sick could be a prayer, if it were offered to God.**"**

Recipe

———≫◆≪———

Quinoa and Lima Bean Patties

Quinoa has been a staple of South American cooking for thousands of years. These healthy patties are inspired by Saint Martin de Porres, who did not eat meat. In addition to quinoa, they contain both tomatoes and limes, which are native to South America. Lovely layers of flavor include sautéed mushrooms and red onions, lime juice and fresh tomatoes, cilantro and cayenne pepper.

- **PREP TIME:** 30 minutes
- **COOK TIME:** 12-15 minutes
- **YIELD:** 5 Large Patties / 10 Small Patties
- **THIS RECIPE IS VEGAN.** Just make sure that you use vegan breadcrumbs, and that your vegetable stock is labeled as vegan. And as always, make sure all ingredients you use are vegan.
- **MAKE IT GLUTEN-FREE** by using gluten-free vegetable stock. Use gluten-free bread-crumbs or make your own by toasting a couple of slices of gluten-free bread and rubbing them with a grater to make crumbs.

INGREDIENTS

1½ cups frozen lima beans (or 1½ cups canned lima beans, rinsed)

2-5 tablespoons olive oil

½ cup chopped red onion (or small red onion)

Sea salt

Ground black pepper

1 clove garlic, finely chopped

½ cup raw tri-color quinoa (or your favorite raw quinoa)

1 cup vegetable stock

8 oz. baby Bella mushrooms, washed, chopped (or your favorite fresh mushroom, washed, chopped)

1 avocado, pit removed, scooped from skin.

1 tablespoon fresh lime juice, and additional lime slices for serving)

1 ripe tomato, chopped (about 6 ounces)

1 tablespoon cilantro leaves, chopped (or fresh parsley, or dried parsley)

1 teaspoon paprika

¼ teaspoon dried cayenne pepper, ground

¼ cup breadcrumbs, plain

DIRECTIONS

- Place frozen lima beans in small pot, cover with water. Bring to boil. Reduce heat and simmer 15 minutes. Drain beans using a sieve or colander and place in large mixing bowl. Mash to a rough mash using the back of a fork (or back of a spoon) or use a food processor with steel blade and pulse a few times until roughly chopped.

- Place 1 tablespoon olive oil in small pot over medium-high heat. Add chopped red onion, ¼ teaspoon sea salt and ⅛ teaspoon black pepper. Stir. Sauté 5 minutes. Add chopped garlic. Sauté another 3 minutes. Add raw, dry quinoa and stir. Sauté 4 minutes. Add vegetable stock. Bring to a boil. Once boiling, reduce heat to simmer. Cover and cook for 12 minutes. Remove from heat when done.

- Heat a large frying pan over medium heat with 1 tablespoon olive oil. Add chopped mushrooms and ¼ teaspoon sea salt and ⅛ teaspoon black pepper. Stir and cover with a lid or baking sheet. Cook 10 minutes, stirring occasionally. Remove from heat; keep covered.

- Add avocado and lime juice to lima beans. Mash avocado well. Add cooked quinoa, sautéed mushrooms, chopped tomato, chopped cilantro (or parsley), paprika, cayenne pepper. Mix well until thoroughly combined. Add breadcrumbs, ¼ teaspoon salt, and ⅛ teaspoon black pepper. Stir well. Taste and adjust seasonings. Let sit for 5 minutes.

- Heat a griddle or two large frying pans (nonstick works best) over medium heat. Add 1 tablespoon olive oil or spray with cooking spray. Measure ½ cup of mixture and shape into a large patty. Or use ¼ cup mixture to make small patties. Cook 6 minutes or until browned. Flip carefully, adding additional oil or cooking spray if needed. Cook 6 minutes on other side. Proceed in subsequent batches, adding oil or cooking spray for each new batch.

- Serving suggestion: Serve with a lime wedge, salad, and a grate of Queso Fresco or your favorite cheese.

Prayers

TRADITIONAL PRAYER

Most humble Martin de Porres, your burning charity embraced not only the poor and needy but even the animals of the field. For your splendid example of charity, we honor you and invoke your help. From your place in heaven, hear the requests of your needy brethren, so that, by imitating your virtues we may live contentedly in that state in which God has placed us. And carrying our cross with strength and courage, may we follow in the footsteps of our blessed Redeemer and his most sorrowful mother, so that at last we may reach the kingdom of heaven through the merits of our Lord Jesus Christ. Amen.

CONTEMPORARY PRAYER

St. Martin, help us to have compassion on all with whom we share this planet, not just our fellow humans, but the animals as well. May we see the face of our Creator in all of God's works. Amen.

CHAPTER 6

St. Kateri Tekakwitha

Martin cautiously opened the kitchen door on his return. Martha pushed a stray hair from her forehead. "Where did you go? Oh, never mind. I got your patties done," she said, holding out a heaping plate. "Might as well put them on the buffet table."

"Thank you so much," Martin said, taking the plate and returning to the main room. He started to set his dish down in the "Main dish" section just as St. Kateri Tekakwitha was placing her dish on the table.

"Oh, excuse me," Martin said. "I didn't mean to take your spot."

"I don't think there are assigned areas," Kateri said. She leaned over and took a long sniff of Martin's quinoa and lima bean patties. "Those smell wonderful!" she said.

"Martha helped make them," Martin admitted. "What about yours?"

"I went for the Three Sisters," Kateri said. "Corn, beans, and squash."

Martin clapped his hands in delight. "Another vegetarian dish! I can't wait to try it." Kateri smiled shyly.

In her earthly life, she used to prepare food for members of her tribe, but she often tried to eat food as flavorless as possible as a penance. In heaven, however, penance wasn't necessary, and Kateri now thoroughly enjoyed eating not only her traditional fare but also new foods as well. She didn't mention to Martin that she had tried John the Baptist's salted locusts—and liked them—since technically speaking locusts aren't vegetarian fare, but then Kateri wasn't a vegetarian.

Just then Teresa of Avila joined them. "Martin," she said. "I have a question for you. It's about my garden. You used to garden, didn't you?"

The Three Sisters is a sacred growing technique developed by Native Americans. Corn provides a structure for bean vines, which in turn add nitrogen to the soil. Squash acts as a groundcover that cuts down on weeds.

• •

Mohawk girls of her age learned how to make clothing from animal hides and household items from reeds and grasses as well as how to cook. Kateri was skilled at these domestic arts. She also was known for her ability to cook traditional foods, including venison.

"A little," he said.

"Good, I want to talk to you about white bougainvillea," she said to Martin, as Kateri wandered away.

Kateri looked up and down the length of the buffet table. It was going to be a feast fit for a king, for sure. She pulled a little tighter the blanket that she always wore and surveyed the room. She used to wear the blanket to cover her smallpox scars, but now she wore it because it was comfortable and comforting.

Kateri wasn't one for chatting. Even on earth, she tended to avoid social gatherings, preferring to sit quietly and watch what was going on around her. *Maybe I should socialize a bit*, she thought. *Or maybe I can just stay here a little longer.* She drew her blanket even closer.

"Are you looking for your place card?" Solanus Casey asked as he came over to her. "It's right over there," he said as he pointed.

"Thank you for letting me know," Kateri said. "Is everyone here?"

"Pretty much," Solanus said. "Except the guest of honor. But we can always wait for the honored guest."

"Yes," she said. "That's one of the perks of being the honored guest."

They stood together in comfortable silence for a few minutes. Then Solanus said, "I've heard that down on earth they are thinking about naming Nicholas Black Elk a saint."

"As if he weren't a saint already," Kateri laughed. "Sometimes down there they act as if they need to make the decision as to who is up here and who isn't."

The Mohawk were nearly wiped out around 1635 by a smallpox epidemic that reduced their population by more than sixty percent. It is estimated that their numbers dropped from just under 8,000 to about 3,000.

. . . .

Nicholas Black Elk, more commonly known simply as Black Elk, was both a medicine man and a holy man of the Oglala Lakota people. He was present at the Battle of the Little Bighorn. He converted to Catholicism in his forties, and the cause for his canonization was opened in 2016. *Black Elk Speaks* by John Neihardt is a popular book about his life and spiritual beliefs, but it doesn't tell the full story of his life, leaving out everything about his conversion to Catholicism and decades spent as a catechist. Check out this new biography instead: *Nicholas Black Elk, Medicine Man, Catechist, Saint*, by Jon M. Sweeney.

"I'd like to see them recognize him. We need them to realize that not everyone up here was a priest or a nun," Solanus said.

"I wanted to be a nun," Kateri said softly, "but I wasn't. It wasn't meant to be."

"No," Solanus said. "And I wasn't a priest. But what I meant was that sometimes people on earth think that only people who dedicated their entire lives to working for the Church can be saints. And that just isn't true," he said emphatically.

"Just another misconception about heaven," Kateri agreed. "But it would be nice to have another Native North American officially recognized. Especially since I lived on the east side of the continent, and Black Elk lived on the west side."

"I pretty much stuck to the middle states," Solanus said. "A lot of time in Indiana and Illinois. Can't say that I miss those winters."

"Tell me about it," Kateri said. "Kahnawake in January could be brutal. Especially when your only heat is a fireplace."

"I've always wanted to know," Solanus said abruptly, changing the subject. "How did you get the nickname 'Lily'?"

Kateri blushed and dropped her head. "It's really sort of embarrassing," she said. "It's because lilies were associated with chastity and dedication to the Virgin. I never married, and I always had a deep devotion to Our Lady. One of the government bureaus wrote a pamphlet that called me 'the fairest flower that ever bloomed among (Native Americans).'" She buried her face in her blanket. "It's really all too much," she said.

"No, it isn't," Solanus said, putting a hand on her shoulder. "You really are a fair flower and you deserve to be called Lily."

Kateri uncovered her face. "You really are too sweet."

"Speaking of sweet," Solanus said with a chuckle. "I happened to make a dessert. I'll bring it out later."

The village of Kahnawake was located on the St. Lawrence River south of what is now Montreal, Quebec, Canada. It is referred to as "on or by the rapids." The French used the area as part of the defense for what would become Montreal and stationed a garrison there. Jesuit records indicate it was settled about 1719.

• • • • • • • • • • • • • • • • • •

The lily has been a symbol of purity and virginity since the Middle Ages. The original pamphlet used a now derogatory term for Native Americans.

Did You Know?

Kateri is named after St. Catherine of Siena.

Kateri is the Mohawk version of Catherine.

In the Lord's Prayer, Jesuit missionaries called heaven by the Mohawk word meaning "Sky World."

⇉ BIOGRAPHY

St. Kateri Tekakwitha

1656 – APRIL 17, 1680

The first Native American to be named a saint, Kateri Tekakwitha was the daughter of Kenneronkwa, a Mohawk chief, and Tagaskouita, an Algonquin woman who had been captured in a raid.

The Mohawks and the Algonquins were traditional enemies. The Mohawks were the easternmost tribe of the Iroquois Confederacy and one of the five original members of the Iroquois League. They were based in the northeastern portion of North America, west of the Hudson River.

Born in what is now western New York State, Kateri was orphaned when she was about four years old when her parents and baby brother were killed in a smallpox epidemic. Left with a badly scarred face and impaired vision, her name, *Tekakwitha*, translates as "she who bumps into things." She was most likely given the nickname because of her poor eyesight. She joined the clan household of her uncle and learned all the traditional skills of the women of her tribe.

Kateri's mother had been baptized by French Jesuit missionaries prior to her capture by the Mohawks, but it is not clear how much she had been able to teach her daughter before her death. When Tekakwitha was eleven years old, the Jesuit missionaries Jacques Frémin, Jacques Bruyas, and Jean Pierron came to her village, but the uncle with whom Kateri lived restricted contact because he did not want his family to become Catholic, although one of his daughters did convert.

When she was about thirteen, her family tried to pressure her into getting married, but she resisted. By the time she was seventeen, her aunts were deeply concerned about her lack of desire for marriage and tried to get her to accept the invitation of a young Mohawk man. Kateri not only refused but also ran away and hid in a field. Eventually, her aunts gave up their attempts to arrange a marriage.

At eighteen, she met the Jesuit priest Jacques de Lamberville, a missionary to the Iroquois, who was a visitor to her village. Because she had an injured foot, she wasn't working with the other women in the fields, so she was able to converse at length with him. During their conversations, she expressed a desire to become a Christian and began to study under his tutelage. She was baptized on Easter Sunday 1676, taking the name Catherine (or Kateri) as her baptismal name.

She remained in her home village for some time but was subject to ridicule and mistreatment by those who opposed her conversion and her determination to lead a holy and abstemious life. Then, on the urging of Fr. Lamberville, she moved to the Jesuit mission of Kahnawake, where her cousin who had become a Catholic had settled.

At Kahnawake, she came under the spiritual guidance of a friend of her mother named Anastasia Tegonhatsiongo, who encouraged Kateri and her close friend Marie Thérèse Tegaianguenta to undertake strenuous penances in reparation for sin. She also fell under the influence of another Jesuit missionary who introduced whips, hair shirts, and iron girdles to the converts living at Kahnawake. Kateri took these self-mortifications very seriously, even inflicting burns on herself. Finally, Marie Thérèse spoke to Fr. Claude Chauchetière, another missionary, who explained that penance should be used in moderation

The Jesuits first arrived in North American in the seventeenth century. They disappeared during the suppression of the Order around 1763 but returned in 1830. Because of continual hostility between the First Nations and the French, the Jesuits faced enormous challenges in trying to spread the gospel. Eight Jesuits are recognized as the North American martyrs: St. René Goupil, St. Isaac Jogues, St. Jean de Lalande, St. Antoine Daniel, St. Jean de Brébeuf, St. Noël Chabanel, St. Charles Garnier, and St. Gabriel Lalemant.

• • • • • • • • • • • • • • • • • • • •

Fr. Claude Chauchetière, the first to write a biography of Kateri in 1695, was the painter of the only known portrait of her done in her lifetime. It shows her in a white tunic with a black blanket over her head. She wears moccasins with yellow laces and is holding a golden crucifix. Fr. Chauchetière came to believe that she was a saint.

and insisted that the young women only perform penances that he approved. Kateri and Marie Thérèse wanted to form a group of women who would live as religious, but they were discouraged because they were "too young in the faith." Instead, the two continued to practice their faith and devotions together.

Kateri's health, never robust after she had smallpox, was dramatically weakened by her penances. During Holy Week 1680, when she was just twenty-four years old, she took a dramatic turn for the worse, and on Holy Wednesday, she was given the last rites. Her friend Marie Thérèse was at her bedside and reported that her last words were "Jesus, Mary, I love you."

She was canonized on October 21, 2012, by Pope Benedict XVI. She is the patron of ecologists, environmentalism, loss of parents, and Native Americans, among others. She is celebrated on July 14.

Legends, Lore, and Miracles

After her death, Kateri is believed to have appeared to her friend Marie-Thérèse Tegaiaguenta, saying, "I've come to say goodbye. I'm on my way to heaven." Fr. Chauchetière claimed that he saw her at her grave in "baroque splendor" with "her face lifted toward heaven as if in ecstasy."

Her face, which had been badly scarred by smallpox, changed dramatically at the time of her death. One of her biographers said that about a quarter of an hour after her death her face "became in a moment so beautiful and so white that I observed it immediately."

In the eighteenth century, a Protestant boy named Joseph Kellogg was believed to have been healed from smallpox after touching a piece of wood from Kateri's coffin. Earth from her gravesite is sometimes worn in pendants and used for cures. The final miracle attributed to Kateri before her canonization happened in 2006 when a young boy from Washington State who was half Lummi was suffering from a flesh-eating bacteria that was killing him; he survived after his parents placed one of Kateri's relics against his body and prayed to her for intercession.

Quote
"Who will teach me what is most pleasing to God, that I may do it?**"**

Recipe

Three Sisters Corn Wraps with Squash, Beans, and Pan-Roasted Corn

Native Americans traditionally grew corn, beans, and squash together. The corn provides a place for the beans to climb. The beans provide nitrogen for the other plants. The large leaves of low-growing squash provide cover to cool the ground, retaining moisture for all to prosper. This powerhouse trio also provides excellent nutritional value.

- **PREP TIME:** 15 minutes
- **COOK TIME:** Vegetables 20-30 minutes; Corn 5 minutes; If using dry beans: 2 hours, 30 minutes combined soak/cook time
- **SERVES:** 6-8 People
- **SERVING SUGGESTIONS:** Serve as a side dish, with warmed tortilla chips, or inside your favorite wrap.
- **THIS RECIPE IS VEGAN AND GLUTEN-FREE.**

INGREDIENTS

2 yellow squash

2 ears fresh corn or 1½ cups frozen corn

1 small can (12-15 oz.) white beans, rinsed and drained well or ½ cup dried small white beans cooked according to directions below

1 medium yellow onion, sliced, then cut slices in half

1 clove garlic, chopped

2 green onions

3 tablespoons olive oil

Salt

Black pepper

DIRECTIONS

Preheat oven to 400 degrees.

If using dry small white beans

- Pick through the beans and discard any discolored beans or foreign items.
- Quick soak the beans: Place beans in small pot. Cover with water. Bring to a boil. Boil for 2 minutes. Move pan off-heat and let sit for 1 hour, covered.
- Cook the beans: Drain the beans after the 1-hour quick soak and return them to the pot. Add enough new water to cover the beans. Add ¼ teaspoon salt, stir. Simmer for 90 minutes, covered.

If using canned beans

- Drain the canned beans and rinse.

Roast the squash, onions, and garlic.

- Clean yellow squash. Cut the ends off. Cut in half lengthwise, then cut each half lengthwise. Cut into ¾-inch slices.
- Cut the root end off green onions, and then cut a couple of inches off the green tops. Cut remaining green onion into thin slices.
- Oil a baking sheet or spray with nonstick cooking spray. Place yellow squash, yellow onions, sliced green onions, and garlic onto baking sheet. Sprinkle with sea salt and black pepper. Drizzle with 2 tablespoons olive oil and toss vegetables to coat in oil. Roast in a 400-degree oven for 10 minutes, then stir. Roast another 10-15 minutes, or until vegetables begin to brown.

Pan-roast the corn kernels.

- Remove husk and any corn silk from corn, rinse under cold water. Hold the corn cob vertically on a cutting board. With a sharp knife, cut the kernels off the cob. Some of each kernel should remain on the cob, otherwise you risk cutting the cob into your kernels.
- Heat a frying pan over high heat. Add 1 tablespoon olive oil. When oil is hot, add the corn kernels to pan. Sprinkle with sea salt and pepper. Stir and spread corn in a layer. Cook one minute or until corn begins to brown. Toss. Cook another minute or two.
- Add beans and roasted vegetables to pan with corn. Cook over medium-high heat until heated throughout. Serve.

Prayers

TRADITIONAL PRAYER

Saint Kateri Tekakwitha, our elder sister in the Lord, discreetly you watch over us; may your love for Jesus and Mary inspire in us words and deeds of friendship, of forgiveness, and of reconciliation. Pray that God will give us the courage, the boldness, and the strength to build a world of justice and peace among ourselves and among all nations. Help us, as you did, to encounter the Creator God present in the very depths of nature, and so become witnesses of Life. With you, we praise the Father, the Son, and the Spirit. Amen. Holy founders of the Church in North America, pray for us.[1]

CONTEMPORARY PRAYER

St. Kateri, you followed your heart and your conscience even when the people around you pressured you to do otherwise. Help us to do what we know is right for us and not be swayed by public pressure. Amen.

CHAPTER 7

St. John Henry Newman

The lean-faced cleric with a shock of white hair stood patiently at the door to the cottage. He had knocked politely, but there had not been an answer. He could hear voices inside, so he knocked again. *I think I've come to the right address*, he said to himself, even though street addresses didn't really exist in heaven. This was St. John Henry Newman's first dinner party in heaven. He was a bit surprised to hear that such things existed, but secretly quite pleased to have been invited since he hadn't been an "official" saint for all that long.

Newman thought back a few days ago when Peter delivered the invitation to the party. "It's not going to be a fancy affair," Peter explained. "Potluck actually."

"Potluck?" Newman asked. "What's that?"

"It's a get-together where the guests bring one of their favorite foods to share. Everyone gets to sample several dishes."

Newman blinked. "Never heard of such a thing. Very odd, if you ask me."

> Newman was canonized by Pope Francis in October 2019. The Irish author James Joyce was a great admirer of Newman's writing.

Peter sighed. "I hadn't heard of it before either, but it's something they do in America. And, well, it seems to have caught on up here."

"Even odder," Newman said.

"Anyway," Peter went on. "It's going to be held over at the thatched cottage just off the Electrum Road. You can't miss it." Newman closed his eyes. Whenever someone said, "You can't miss it," it was sure to be extraordinarily hard to find. "Just bring something you liked to eat when you were down on earth. I'm bringing fish," Peter added.

"Naturally," Newman nodded. "And what is the occasion for this 'potluck'?"

"It's a surprise party, more or less," Peter said. "Not that there are exactly surprises up here. It's a gathering to honor a 'special guest.'"

"Ah, I see. So there will be bread and wine, too?"

Peter flashed a broad, toothy grin. "Couldn't have a party without them."

After Peter left, Newman went to a small, book-lined office at the back of his house. He sank into an overstuffed leather chair and picked up a poem he had been working on since he had arrived. He was having trouble with the third stanza. *Not nearly as good as "Pillar of the Cloud,"* he thought.

Newman first wrote the hymn "Lead, Kindly Light" as a poem entitled "Pillar of the Cloud," which was published in the *British Magazine* in 1834 and republished in *Lyra Apostolica* in 1836. He wrote it while the ship he was sailing on was becalmed at sea for a week in the Straits of Bonifacio.

• • • • • • • • • • • • • • • • • • • •

John Newman and Ambrose St. John lived together as friends for thirty-two years and were buried in a common grave, according to Newman's wishes. He wrote: "I wish, with all my heart, to be buried in Fr Ambrose St John's grave — and I give this as my last, my imperative will." They share a marker with the words: *Ex umbris et imaginibus in veritatem* ("Out of shadows and phantasms into the truth"). In 2008, the Church decided to relocate Newman's remains, as per usual practice when someone is about to be declared a saint, but there were no remains left. He had apparently been buried without a lead coffin, and all that was there were artifacts of his that were buried with the body.

A noise outside the room made him look up. "Ambrose," he said. "You startled me." Newman and Ambrose St. John shared a house in heaven, just as they had shared one on earth. Newman tucked the poem under a book. He wasn't ready to reveal it publicly quite yet, not even to his good friend. He wondered if they had poetry readings in heaven, since they had dinner parties. He would need to check into that.

"I ran into Peter as he was leaving. Said something about an invitation," Ambrose said.

"We've been invited to a dinner party. A 'potluck,'" Newman added. "It's a sort of bring-your-own-food affair as far as I can tell."

"Probably an American invention," Ambrose sniffed.

"Indeed," Newman agreed. "The invitation included you. Do you want to come?

Ambrose shook his head vehemently. "No, no," he protested. "I'll be just fine here with my books."

"As would I," Newman said, "But I don't think we can both decline an invitation from Peter. So, the next question is 'What shall I bring?'" His blue eyes twinkled. "It's got to be very British . . . and perhaps a bit unexpected. No Yorkshire pudding. Too predictable."

"And too hard to transport. Would collapse before you got it to table," Ambrose said. "Unless you were planning on levitating it. What about Bubble and Squeak?"

"That's more of a breakfast food and this is a dinner. Not to mention I'm not sure I should bring cabbage. Gas, you know." Newman wrinkled his brow. "I've got it! Toad in the Hole!"

"Shall I look for a real toad in the garden?" Ambrose joked.

"That might be taking the idea of luck at a pot a bit too far," Newman said. "No, I'll just make the regular version with sausage. Do we have the right sized pan for it?" he asked.

"I'll check," Ambrose said.

> Bubble and Squeak is a traditional British breakfast food made with potatoes and cabbage. It gets its name because the cabbage makes a bubbling or squeaking noise during cooking.
>
> •
>
> St. Francis Solanus was a Spanish missionary to South America in the early seventeenth century.

Ambrose found a pan and helped Newman make Toad in the Hole. Now at the party, with his hot dish in hand, Newman knocked a third time at the cottage door. He hadn't quite learned that everything in heaven happened in threes yet. This time, the door swung open and there, before him, was Solanus Casey.

"Come on in," Solanus said, opening the door wide. "The party is just getting started."

"I've been meaning to look you up," Newman said apologetically. "But I'm learning that heaven is a bit like retirement. There are so many things to keep you occupied you don't know where the time goes. Well, not that there is time here," he said almost sheepishly.

"I completely understand," Solanus said. "I keep thinking that I should get together with my namesake, St. Francis Solanus, but it never seems to happen." The two entered the room. "Put your dish over there," Solanus said, pointing at the table. "I assumed Peter explained the notion of a potluck to you."

"Indeed," Newman said. He started to cross the room to put his dish with other main dishes when St. Augustine of Hippo approached him.

"So glad to see you here," Augustine said. "I've been meaning to look you up." Solanus and Newman gave each other a knowing look. "I don't mean to be pushy, but before the party gets going, may I offer you a bit of advice? Not to offend, but you are a relative newcomer, I mean in terms of canonization on earth."

"Of course." Newman placed his Toad in the Hole on the edge of the table and blinked expectantly.

"This is something I've learned since I've been up here," Augustine continued. "I know you spent a lot of time on earth writing about points of theology and the differences between various groups of Christians." Newman nodded. "I did the same in my day. There's really nothing new under the sun. And while I do understand the importance of correct dogma and proper theology, up here those differences really aren't all that important. If you want to keep exploring the variations of doctrine, that's perfectly fine. You really can do whatever it is you want up here—within reason," he added with a chuckle. "But if you want my suggestion, just let yourself be. Let the folks on earth talk about theology. Up here, we just live it. I know you liked to take long walks, so take walks. You can walk as long as you like up here and see anything you want." He leaned closer to Newman. "And while we don't advertise it, you can always pay a quick trip back to earth. Just be careful. People on earth get nervous if they spot us. If it's a Catholic who sees you, they may think it's a holy visitation, but the rest of them will just think they've seen a ghost."

"So 'I must show what I am, that it may be seen what I am not,'" Newman quoted himself. "Lest they think I am a phantom 'dressed up in my clothes.'"

> "I must show what I am, that it may be seen what I am not, and the phantom extinguished which gibbers instead of me. I wish to be known as a living man, and not as a scarecrow which is dressed up in my clothes."
> *Apologia Pro Vita Sua*

"Exactly right," Augustine said. "But you might enjoy dropping by Oxford. Or even checking in on some of the Newman Centers in America. University life has changed some since you were teaching, but youth remains youth, and universities remain universities no matter when or where they are."

The two former professors exchanged knowing nods. "If you will excuse me," Augustine said. "Francis Borgia is waiting for me." He pointed to the Jesuit standing beside a window on the far side of the room. "Perhaps we can talk later."

Newman Centers, which are ministry centers at many public and private institutions of higher learning, are named after Cardinal Newman. The first center/house was established in 1888 at Oxford. The first American Newman Club was founded in 1893 at the University of Pennsylvania. There are more than 2,000 Newman Centers in the United States.

Did You Know?

John Henry Newman lived at the same time as the English Romantic poets John Keats and Percy Bysshe Shelley.

⇒ BIOGRAPHY

St. John Henry Newman

FEBRUARY 21, 1801 – AUGUST 11, 1890

John Henry Newman is arguably the most famous Anglican convert to Catholicism in modern times. His long life spanned a fascinating time in history in the West. He was alive to see Great Britain become the dominant power in the world, Thomas Jefferson become president of the United States, the first steam locomotives start hauling passengers and freight, Beethoven perform his Fifth Symphony, Napoleon suffer defeat at Waterloo, and *Jane Eyre* be published.

The son of a London banker, Newman was sent to study at Great Ealing School at age seven, where he read the works of political theorist Thomas Paine and philosopher David Hume, as well as the novels of Walter Scott. Newman became an evangelical Calvinist at age fifteen, writing in his famous work *Apologia* that he was more certain of his faith "than that I have hands or feet." Throughout his life, he considered that initial conversion experience as a high point of the spiritual journey that eventually led him to the Catholic Church.

There are only five official saints who came from London. In addition to Newman, they include Thomas More, Thomas Becket, Edmund Campion, and Polydore Plasden.

• •

The Oxford Movement, centered at the university from which it derived its name, attempted a renewal of "Catholic" practices within the Church of England, arguing that the Anglican denomination had been "catholic" since the beginning. One of the arguments was that Anglican bishops were in direct "apostolic succession," that is, they could trace their lineage back to the Apostles. The basic tenets of the movement were outlined in a series of ninety *Tracts for the Times*, twenty-four of which were written by Newman.

In 1824, he became an Anglican deacon and was ordained a priest in May 1825. For seventeen years, he served as vicar at St. Mary the Virgin University Church as well as serving as a tutor at Oriel College. Gradually, he came to study the early Church Fathers, and this led to his involvement in the Oxford Movement.

Eventually, his studies led him to question whether Anglican theology was consistent with the principles of ecclesiastical authority he had encountered in his studies of the Church Fathers. After much soul-searching, in which he tried to defend the "middle way" of Anglicanism between Catholicism and Protestantism, Newman finally concluded that the Roman Catholic Church was, indeed, the church founded by Jesus Christ.

A few more years passed before Newman converted to Catholicism. He entered the Church on October 9, 1845. In February 1846, he was ordained a Catholic priest and was awarded the degree of Doctor of Divinity by Pope Pius IX. Returning to England, he finally settled at Edgbaston, a suburb of Birmingham, where he lived a mostly secluded life for the next forty years (except for a few years in Ireland).

A prolific author, Newman wrote dozens of books and more than 21,000 letters that still survive. Many volumes of his sermons were also published after his death. His most famous works include his *Apologia Pro Vita Sua* (his spiritual autobiography), *Essay on the Development of Christian Doctrine, On Consulting the Faithful in Matters of Doctrine,* and *Essay on the Grammar of Assent.*

In 1879, Pope Leo XIII named Newman a cardinal. Newman accepted the honor on two conditions: first, that he not be named a bishop as was customary because he did not want the duties of that rank, and second, that he be allowed to remain at Edgbaston. The Pope agreed.

Newman continued to write and study until his health began to fail, and he celebrated Mass for the last time on Christmas 1889. He died of pneumonia on August 11, 1890. He was canonized in 2019. No official patronages have been assigned, but students around the world honor him as one of their patrons.

Ordinarily, a saint's feast day is the day of their death, but August 11 has already been claimed by St. Clare of Assisi. Therefore, October 9 was assigned to Newman because, as the Liturgy Office of England and Wales explains—"it falls at the beginning of the University year; an area in which Newman had a particular interest."

Legends, Lore, and Miracles

While it is not known if Newman read Charles Darwin's *On the Origin of Species*, which was published while Newman was teaching, both men explored the idea of change and development in humanity—Newman on the spiritual side, Darwin on the physical. Newman wrote, "To live is to change and to be perfect is to have changed often."

In 2001, Jack Sullivan, an American deacon from Marshfield in Massachusetts, attributed his recovery from a spinal cord disorder to the intercession of Newman. The miracle was used for Newman's beatification.

A second miracle attributed to Newman's intercession involved a woman with three small children who was diagnosed with a subchorionic hematoma, a blood clot in the fetal membrane during a pregnancy. Bedrest is the only treatment, and the risk of miscarriage as well as maternal death is high. When the mother began to bleed, she called out, "Cardinal Newman, please stop the bleeding." The bleeding stopped immediately, and the pregnancy continued without incident. The woman went on to have two other children.

Quote
"*Cor ad cor loquitur*"
—"Heart speaks unto heart."

Recipe

━━━◆◆◆◆◆━━━

Toad in the Hole

Since Toad in the Hole was first mentioned as early as 1762, where it was called "meat boiled in a crust," it's likely Newman would have eaten it at some time. Its name may refer to the way that toads hide in holes waiting for prey, something like the sausages hide in the batter.

- **PREP TIME:** 10 minutes, plus 1 hour to rest batter
- **COOK TIME:** Brown Sausages (10-15 minutes) plus bake time (25-30 minutes)
- **SERVES:** 6

INGREDIENTS

1¼ cups flour	Pinch of black pepper
1 cup eggs, beaten (4-5 eggs, approximately)	5-7 large or 10-12 smaller link sausages
¾ cup milk, room temperature	½ teaspoon canola oil or corn oil
¼ cup club soda/seltzer or water	2 tablespoons butter
½ teaspoon salt	

DIRECTIONS

- Make the batter:

  Place flour, salt and pepper in a medium bowl, whisk to combine. Add the beaten eggs and whisk until smooth. Add the milk in 4 additions, whisking after each addition. Then add club soda or water. Whisk to combine.

- Rest the Batter:

  Cover the bowl with plastic wrap or a clean kitchen towel and allow batter to rest at room temperature for an hour. You may make in advance and refrigerate for up to 24 hours. Just be sure to have batter at room temperature when you are ready to bake your Toad in the Hole.

- Brown the sausages in a pan on stovetop. Remove from pan and set aside.

- Make the Toad in the Hole:
  Preheat oven to 450 degrees. Place oven rack in lower third of oven.

- Choice of pan:
  Since you are working with such a hot oven, choose a metal baking pan – such as a 9" round cake pan, a 9" or 10" square cake pan, or similar size cast iron skillet with sides at least 3" high.
- Grease your baking pan with the Canola or Corn oil. (Note: You need an oil with a high smoke point—not olive oil, coconut oil or any oil that will not withstand 450 degrees.)
- When batter is fully rested and at room temperature, place butter in your pan and place pan in 450-degree oven for 2 minutes, or until butter is melted and sizzling. Do not let the butter brown. Remove the pan from oven and pour batter into the pan carefully—it might splatter from the hot butter combining with the batter. Then place sausages on top of batter in pan in whatever arrangement you like; sausages should be spaced apart.
- Place pan back in the oven quickly. Bake for 15 minutes, checking halfway through. If you find that one side is puffing up more than the other side, rotate your pan. After 15 minutes at 450 degrees, reduce oven to 400 degrees. Continue baking for 10-15 minutes, or until top center is medium golden brown. Serve at once, as it deflates quickly.

Prayers

TRADITIONAL PRAYER

May the Lord support us all the day long,
Till the shades lengthen and the evening comes,
and the busy world is hushed, and the fever of life is over,
and our work is done.
Then in his mercy may he give us a safe lodging,
and holy rest, and peace at the last. Amen.

CONTEMPORARY PRAYER

May we, like you, St. John Henry Newman, always recognize that we have
a job to do and a role to play in God's plan for humanity. Help us see that
job and have the courage to fulfill it. Amen.

CHAPTER 8

St. Augustine of Hippo

No sooner had Augustine joined Francis Borgia when they were in a heated discussion. After thirty minutes of back and forth, Augustine said, "I think we are going to have to agree to disagree about this. It's not like either of us played either sport in our earthly lives."

"That's true," Borgia agreed. "But you can't deny that soccer is more popular around the world than American football."

"Conceded," Augustine said.

"I suppose I should go check on my pesto pasta," Borgia said. "The pesto needs some last-minute preparation. I tried to get Martha to do it for me, but she said something about helping one saint with his cooking was quite enough for her."

"Good luck," Augustine said. "I brought oxtail soup. All I needed to do was make sure that it was kept warm."

> The name Augustine is derived from the Roman word *august* meaning great or noble. *Hippo* is the Greek word for horse. Thus, Augustine is a Great One from Horse. (Hippopotamus literally means "river horse" in Greek.)

As Borgia meandered back toward the kitchen, Augustine pushed open the shutters on the window behind him and looked out at the expansive fruit orchard. He felt what might have been a twinge of long-forgotten guilt as he looked at the various varieties of fruit—apples, pears, peaches, plums—all ripe and ready for the picking, remembering how, when he was a boy, he and some friends stole fruit, not out of hunger but because it was forbidden. *Perhaps I should have made an apple pie . . . in reparation,* he thought, but immediately he dismissed the idea. It was hard enough slipping down the back ways of heaven trying to avoid "her" with a pot of soup under his robe, much less a fresh-baked pie. She could smell pie a mile away . . . if there were miles in heaven. And she was sure to remind him of that fruit incident if he had a pie with him. *She has a memory like an elephant,* he thought.

When he had arrived at the party slightly out of breath, Solanus had asked him what was wrong. "Mother," Augustine said, looking over his shoulder, and Solanus quickly ushered him in. It wasn't that Augustine didn't love his mother, Monica. This was heaven, after all, and it was impossible not to love. And he loved her dearly when they were on earth. Her death was one of the hardest times of his life. It was just that his mother was, well, a bit difficult. Even now she wanted to make sure she knew what exactly what he was doing all the time, which was a challenge since technically speaking there isn't any time in heaven. He once told a friend that while people thought he had said, "Lord, make me chaste, but not yet," what he was really thinking was, *Lord, don't make me chased by my mother, at least not yet.*

When Augustine was trying to leave Carthage for Rome, he reports, "She was hanging onto me coercively, trying to either stop my journey or come along with me on it." He told her he was visiting a friend and was able to escape . . . for a while. A few years later, she arrived in Milan to join him.

• •

While moderns think of a concubine as a mistress or even a prostitute, in Augustine's time such a woman would be more like a common-law wife. If a man of higher rank fell in love with a woman of lower rank, marriage would have been impossible. So the couple may have lived together in a monogamous union for many years, even for a lifetime. Augustine might have done the same if his mother hadn't insisted on ending the union so he could make a suitable marriage.

Monica would have been welcome at the party, of course, since everyone was always welcome, but Augustine was just as glad that she had taken it upon herself to be a greeter to new arrivals. She had often brought offerings to churches when she was alive, and now she was sort of a one-woman Welcome Wagon to heaven, happily instructing new arrivals on the whats and whatfors of heavenly etiquette while handing out the halos and harps they always seemed to want at first and then discarded after a few days.

As he looked out the window, Augustine's mind began to wander to other gardens he had known. He thought of the shady garden in Milan where he first heard the words "Take up and read" and then recalled the oasis garden in Carthage where he had spent so many happy hours with his concubine, the mother of his son.

Not long after he arrived in the celestial realms, he looked her up. "I'm sorry," he said. "I'm sorry I hurt you."

She smiled at him, a gentle, knowing smile, and touched his hand. "I know. It wasn't entirely your fault. Your mother did have a little something to do with it."

Augustine dropped his head. "Yes, but I should have followed my heart. I should never have allowed my mother to try to force me into a marriage I didn't want."

"No," his concubine said. "But we all make mistakes. And we do have a wonderful son."

"We do," Augustine agreed. "Adeodatus is a true gift from God. You know, he has taken it upon himself to teach newcomers that love is more important than any specific doctrine. It isn't always easy. So many come here thinking it was their adherence to dogma that got them here and not divine mercy."

"I know. I'm so proud of him."

"As am I," he hesitated. "I'm proud of you, too. You always were stronger than me. You made the sacrifice of our relationship with a courage and generosity I could never have imitated."

"It wasn't easy, but I came to accept it," she said. "I always knew that you loved me. And that you still do."

That was the last time Augustine had talked with her. It wasn't that he actively avoided her, as he sometimes did his mother; they simply moved in different celestial circles. Lately, he spent most of his time talking with some Neanderthals about the development of faith and how early hominids fit with the story of Adam and Eve. Adeodatus's mother, on the other hand, spent much of her time with women of "ill repute" who were quite surprised to have found themselves in heaven.

His exact words are: "She was stronger than I and made her sacrifice with a courage and generosity which I was not strong enough to imitate."

• •

Augustine's book *The Literal Meaning of Genesis* aimed at discussing "the scriptures according to their proper meaning of what actually happened." He believed that because the Bible was divinely authored, it is also scientifically correct. Scientists now believe that Neanderthals may have practiced some kinds of ceremonial rituals, although we have no way of knowing what, if any, religious beliefs they might have held. In one interesting piece of evidence, Neanderthal sites in Iraq show evidence of purposeful, ritual burial. The individual in one grave, Shanidar 4, may even have been buried with flowers.

Augustine's memorial reverie was cut short when he spotted a dark-haired woman striding purposefully down the street toward the Pearly Gates. Behind her, a guardian angel, his wings looking a little droopy, was hauling an enormous cart brimming over with baskets of halos and harps.

Monica was in the habit of taking porridge, bread, water, and wine to certain churches in memory of the saints. When she was in Milan, the bishop Ambrose forbade her to bring wine, so she brought "a heart full of purer petitions" and gave "all that she could to the poor."

Slamming the shutters with a bang, Augustine turned his back to the window. *Teresa is right,* he thought. *There is a time for penance and a time for partridge and now is the time for partridge. I'll deal with Mother a little later.*

Did You Know?

Augustine was about age eighteen when his only child was born.

St. Augustine of Hippo

NOVEMBER 13, 354 – AUGUST 28, 430

*A*ugustine is one of the most famous of the early Church Fathers. His writings have influenced Christian thought and teaching for nearly 2,000 years. He was born in the Roman province of Numidia in what is now Algeria; his mother, Monica, was a pious Christian. His pagan father, Patricius, is said to have converted on his deathbed.

When Augustine was about seventeen, he was sent to Carthage to continue his education in rhetoric, or the art of persuasion. This was one of three arts of discourse taught in ancient times, the other two being grammar and logic.

He admits that he lived a licentious and hedonistic lifestyle at the time. It was also in Carthage that he began living with the mother of his son, a relationship that lasted at least fifteen years, and it was there that he became a Manichaean, over his mother's strenuous objections.

After finishing his education, he remained in Carthage teaching rhetoric but grew restless and traveled to Rome where he thought he could find more enthusiastic students. Eventually, he moved to Milan, where he met Bishop Ambrose of Milan, an encounter that changed his life forever. A prolific writer, Ambrose is (like Augustine himself) one of the Doctors of the Church, and he, along with Monica, who had followed Augustine to Milan, helped convince Augustine to consider Christianity as the one true religion.

Augustine was a Berber, at least on his mother's side. Berbers are the indigenous people of North Africa. Their traditional lands cover Morocco, Algeria, Tunisia, Libya, and Mauritania, as well as part of Mali, Niger, and Egypt. His family was deeply influenced by Roman culture, but he acknowledged his African ancestry, writing of one man as "a countryman of ours, insofar as being African."

• •

Manichaeism is a dualistic religious belief dependent on special knowledge of spiritual truths. In that regard, it was a form of Gnosticism. Its teachings are complex, but basically, it espouses that spirit and matter, good and evil, light and dark, are in fundamental opposition to each other. It was condemned as a heresy by the early Church.

It was during their time in Milan that Monica insisted Augustine send the mother of his son back to Africa and arranged a marriage for him with a ten-year-old girl from a suitable family. His son, Adeodatus, remained with him and Monica in Milan. Since he had to wait for two years until his fiancée became of marriageable age, Augustine took another mistress, making his famous statement, "Grant me chastity and continence, but not yet." He eventually gave up his second mistress and broke up his engagement in favor of celibacy and eventual ordination.

Augustine never really got over the loss of his first concubine, seeming to have equated their relationship to marriage. He wrote, "being plucked away from my side, my heart, cleaving unto her, was broken by this means, and wounded, yea, and blood drawn from it."

• • • • • • • • • • • •

Augustine was fluent in Latin, since it was his first language, but he never became proficient in Greek. His original Greek teacher was a harsh taskmaster, and Augustine rebelled by not studying.

On Easter Sunday 387, Augustine and Adeodatus were baptized by Ambrose. A year later, as Monica, Augustine, and Adeodatus were awaiting a ship to return to Africa, Monica died. Not long after landing in Africa, Adeodatus died as well. Augustine then sold his property, except for the family home, which he kept as a monastery for himself and others. He was ordained a priest at Hippo and eventually was named bishop of that area as well, living there until his death in 410.

One of Augustine's most famous books is his *Confessions* in which he details his own early life and conversion as well as penning philosophical reflections on free will and other topics. In it, he recounts hearing a child's voice telling him to "take up and read." Opening the Bible at random he read, "not in rioting and drunkenness, not in chambering and wantonness, not in strife and envying, but put on the Lord Jesus Christ, and make no provision for the flesh to fulfill the lusts thereof" (Rom. 13:13–14.) His famous prayer that begins "Late have I love Thee" is taken from his *Confessions*. Another Augustinian classic is *The City of God*. It covers such diverse topics as free will, original sin, suffering, and the presence of evil. *The City of God* also sets out to demonstrate that Christianity was not to blame for the fall of the Roman Empire.

He died on August 28, 430, and was named a Doctor of the Church in 1298. He is the patron of brewers, printers, and theologians and is invoked for aid with eye ailments.

Legends, Lore, and Miracles

Augustine is often portrayed with a book, which is understandable, but in the Middle Ages it became popular to show him with a heart that is on fire or pierced by an arrow. This may have been because in *Confessions 9, 2.3*, he writes: "You have pierced our heart with your love, and we carried your words embedded in our vital organs." In any event, we have no indication that Augustine was ever shot with a real arrow.

When the Vandals burned the city of Hippo, they left Augustine's cathedral and library unscathed.

The most famous legend associated with Augustine is "The Child by the Seaside." The story goes as follows:

> While Augustine was pondering how God could be three Persons in one God, he decided to walk along the shore. He met a child who had dug a hole in the sand and was scooping water from the sea into the hole with a seashell. Augustine asked him what he was doing, and the child said that he was putting all the water from the sea into the hole in the sand. Augustine told him that was impossible, for the sea was too big and the hole too small. In reply, the child said that it would be more likely for Augustine to put the sea in the hole than it would be for him to comprehend the mysteries of the Trinity. Augustine looked away for a moment, and in that instant the child disappeared.

Augustine was not known for performing miracles, but he is said to have cured a sick man during the siege of Hippo in the spring of 430.

Quote
"The world is a book, and those who do not travel read only a page."

Recipe

————◆————

Oxtail Soup

Oxtail soup is a classic Roman stew and one that Augustine might have eaten during his stay in Italy. Oxtails create a deliciously rich broth while cooking, and yield tender, shredded beef. Rich tones of red wine and coffee work with the aromatics to round out this hearty, flavorful dish. This soup is also wonderful with the addition of cooked barley.

- **PREP TIME:** 30 minutes
- **COOK TIME:** 4–4½ hours
- **SERVES: 10-12.** Leftovers may be refrigerated up to 3 days, or frozen in an airtight container for up to 6 months.
- **NOTE:** If you have purchased frozen oxtails, defrost in refrigerator for 24-48 hours before cooking them. You will likely purchase oxtails that have already been cut into pieces. If not, ask your butcher to cut them into pieces for you.
- **MAKE IT GLUTEN-FREE** by using gluten-free beef broth. Substitute corn starch or your favorite gluten-free gravy thickener for the flour. Eliminate the Worcestershire sauce. Make sure your wine, tomato paste, and coffee are labeled as gluten-free. Check that your oxtails have not been processed with any gluten products.

INGREDIENTS

1 leek

3 pounds oxtails, trimmed and cut into 3"-5" pieces, trimmed of fat and any thick outer layer if possible.

¾ teaspoon sea salt or kosher salt, divided

Ground black pepper (¼ tsp + ⅛ tsp)

1-2 tablespoons cooking oil (example: canola)

1 yellow onion, diced

6 carrots, peeled and sliced into ¼" slices

6 stalks celery, cleaned, cut into ½" slices

2 cloves garlic, chopped

2 tablespoons flour

1 cup dry red wine

¼ cup tomato paste

2 quarts beef stock or beef broth

¼ cup brewed strong coffee

1 teaspoon Worcestershire sauce

2 bay leaves

¼ cup fresh chopped parsley, or 2 tablespoons dried parsley

½ teaspoon dried thyme, or 1½ teaspoons fresh chopped thyme leaves

DIRECTIONS

- Cut off the root end and the green, leafy end from the leek; discard. Cut leek in half lengthwise. Slice each half of leek into ¼ slices and place slices in a bowl of cold water. Move leek slices around with your hands to remove any sand or grit. Remove leek slices from water with your hands, shake over sink, and place on paper towels to drain.

- Season the oxtails with ¼ teaspoon salt and ⅛ teaspoon pepper. Heat a large, heavy pot over medium-high heat. Add 1½ tablespoons cooking oil. Brown the oxtails, turning as needed to brown evenly on all sides. Work in batches, if necessary, to not overcrowd the pan, adding oil to the pan for subsequent batches. Set the browned oxtails aside on a dish, then blot excess oil with paper towels.

- Working in the same pan, add the onion and leeks. Cook over medium-high heat until the onion is softened and begins to turn light brown, about 8 minutes. Add additional cooking oil to the pan if needed.

- Add the carrots and celery to the pan. Add ½ teaspoon salt and ¼ teaspoon pepper and more cooking oil if needed. Cook, stirring occasionally, until celery begins to soften, about 8 minutes. Add garlic and cook while stirring, until garlic appears softened, about 2-3 minutes. Do not brown the garlic.

- Add flour to the pan and stir to coat flour with any oil in the pan. Whisk in the wine, tomato paste, and 1 quart beef stock, scraping the bottom of the pan and whisking to remove any lumps. Cook 10 minutes over medium-high heat, stirring occasionally so as not to burn.

- Add to pot: Oxtails, remaining 1 quart of beef stock, coffee, and Worcestershire sauce. Bring just to a boil, then reduce heat to simmer. Skim off any foam from surface and discard. Add the herbs: Bay leaves, parsley and thyme, and stir to combine. Cover pot and simmer for 3-3½ hours, until the meat in the oxtail can be easily pierced with a fork and the fork can be removed without any resistance.

- Skim fat from surface of soup and discard. Remove bay leaves. Remove oxtails from pot with tongs or slotted spoon. Remove meat from bones when cool enough to handle. Rough chop the meat and add to soup. Discard bones. Note: Removing the fat from the soup is easier if refrigerated overnight. It will rise to the top and solidify – simply spoon the fat off and discard.

Prayers

TRADITIONAL PRAYER

Late have I loved Thee, O Lord; and behold,
Thou wast within and I without, and there I sought Thee.
Thou wast with me when I was not with Thee.
Thou didst call, and cry, and burst my deafness.
Thou didst gleam, and glow, and dispel my blindness.
Thou didst touch me, and I burned for Thy peace.
For Thyself Thou hast made us,
And restless our hearts until in Thee they find their ease.
Late have I loved Thee, Thou Beauty ever old and ever new

CONTEMPORARY PRAYER

St. Augustine, help me find the courage to do what I know is right, regardless of the pressures of family or society. May I be honest with myself and with all those who come in contact with me. Amen.

CHAPTER 9

St. Josephine Margaret Bahkita

J osephine Bahkita sat quietly on a bench at the side of the room, watching as people milled about, making conversation. She smiled when someone looked her way, but otherwise she remained still and calm, preferring to observe rather than participate. Noticing her sitting alone, Augustine approached. "Are you well?," he asked, before remembering that one cannot be anything but well in heaven.

"Most sure," she said softly. "I was just watching the people. I enjoy people watching, don't you?"

"People are fascinating," Augustine agreed. "I'm told that you are from Africa," he said suddenly. "You know I'm from North Africa."

"Yes, I knew that," she said. "I am from Darfur. But I lived most of my adult life in Italy. I lived there so long many people seem to think that I was from Italy."

Augustine sat down on the bench beside Josephine and adjusted his white, toga-like robes. "I have a similar problem. Even though I spent most of my life in Africa, people think that I am Roman or Italian. All because I was a disciple of Ambrose of Milan. But I am and always was a proud African."

"Once I left Africa, I never was able to return," Josephine said with a touch of sadness in her voice. "But my heart always remained there."

"That's what I wanted to talk to you about," Augustine said. "I heard that you were a wonderful speaker, and the young nuns always loved to hear you tell stories about your life."

Josephine was from the Daju, who are believed to have been related to the people who ruled Egypt as the Black Pharaohs in the 25th Egyptian Dynasty from 774-656 BC. The Daju migrated from the Nile Valley around the middle of the fourth century after Christ to Darfur, an area in western Sudan. An independent sultanate for many years, it was incorporated into Sudan in 1916. Darfur has been involved in a major armed conflict since 2003, when the Sudan Liberation Movement and the Justice and Equality Movement began fighting the government of Sudan. A campaign of ethnic cleansing of non-Arabs has resulted in hundreds of thousands of deaths. Peace negotiations have been elusive.

One of Josephine's principal duties between 1935–1939 was to travel around Italy helping prepare missionaries, especially sisters in her own Canossian communities, for missionary work in Africa. She usually told the sisters about her childhood and how she came to be a Christian. Her talks were very popular, and the story of her life, *Storia meravigliosa* by Ida Zanolini, published in 1931, made her famous throughout Italy.

• • • • • • • • • • • • • • • • • •

Although this particular tale comes from South Sudan and Josephine was from Western Sudan, it is a typical piece of Sudanese folklore.

"So I am told," she said modestly. "I enjoyed talking about the Lord, but I also enjoyed telling about my own life. I think I learned how to tell stories by listening to the tales my mother used to tell us as children."

"I would be pleased if you would tell one to me now," Augustine said.

Josephine thought for a moment. "There is one called the Woman and the Rat that is very famous in my part of the world." She composed herself and began to tell the story. Her dark eyes began to shine, and for a moment, it was if she were transported back to her home, to Olgoassa, a region near Mount Agilerei.

"It is the story of how rats and people came to live together," she began. "Once upon a time Rat lived very far from people. At this time, when women were ready to give birth, they had their stomachs cut open. Each time the woman would die but the child would live. One day Rat came to the village and asked why all the women who were pregnant were killed at the time of delivery. He asked that the villagers call him the next time a woman went into labor."

By now, a small group had gathered around and was listening intently as the gentle sister wove her tale. "When the time of birth arrived, Rat was informed. As the labor pains grew more intense, the villagers wanted to cut open the stomach of the woman and take out the baby. Rat stopped them saying, 'No. Be patient. The baby will come.' After many hours, the woman delivered her baby. She could not believe that she was alive because all the women she had known were killed when their babies were born. She cried out, 'Is it true that Rat saved my life? Is it true that Rat did not let my stomach be cut open?' When she was told it was true, she said that she would give Rat whatever he wanted in return for saving her life. One village suggested that Rat be given a cow with a calf, but Rat said politely, 'No, thank you.' Another suggested that Rat might want the newborn baby but again Rat said, No, thank you.' The people wondered why Rat was refusing such generous gifts."

Josephine looked up and to her surprise, the entire room was quietly listening to her. "Continue," Augustine encouraged. "We all want to hear the ending."

Josephine composed herself and continued. "Rat said, 'If you were to give me these gifts, I could not take care of them. But I have an idea. If the women in the village would allow me to stay near their homes and let me share your food, I would be grateful. The women of the village agreed, and that is why to this day Rat and his family are allowed to live near our homes, and the women do not kill them."

As Josephine finished her story, a voice came from the back of the room. "I guess it's a good thing I didn't live in Sudan." Gertrude of Nivelles gave a slight sniffle. "I never would allow rats or mice in my monastery."

Josephine looked up and smiled kindly. "I was never all that fond of them myself, but that is the story my people tell."

"Good thing there aren't any rats or mice here," Gertrude continued. "I, for one, would make sure they were sent far away." At the back of the room, Martin tucked Squeaky a little deeper into his sleeve.

"Thank you," Augustine said as the group dispersed. "That was a delightful story."

Josephine nodded. "Fairy tales are fun, but I would hear about your conversion. Tell me, how was it that you first came to know the Lord?"

"It's a bit of a long story," Augustine said.

"So tell me as much as you can before our honored guest arrives," she said softly. "I want to know."

Did You Know?

Josephine was called *Sor Moretta* ("little brown sister") or *Madre Moretta* ("black mother").

Margaret was one of the names that Josephine took at her baptism, when she was about twenty years old.

❖ BIOGRAPHY

St. Josephine Margaret Bakhita
1869 – February 8, 1947

Josephine Bakhita was born around 1869 into a family of seven children, including a twin sister. The village they lived in is thought to have been located a few miles southwest of Khartoum. Her father was the brother of the village chief, and Josephine's childhood was a happy one until the day when tragedy struck. Her older sister was kidnapped into slavery while the rest of the family were working in the fields. Then, when Josephine was about nine years old, she and a friend were picking herbs when she herself was kidnapped by the same Arab slave traders who had abducted her older sister.

Forced to walk barefoot nearly 600 miles, she was bought and sold twice before arriving at El Obeid, the capital of the state of North Kurdufan in Sudan. She was so traumatized that when she was asked her name, she couldn't answer, so the slave traders called her "Bakhita," an Arabic word that means "lucky" or "fortunate," in an attempt to mock and insult her.

At El Obeid, she was purchased by her third owner, an Arab who used her as a maid for his daughters. While the family treated her relatively well, when she broke a vase, one of the owner's sons beat her so severely that she was unable to leave her bed for a month before being sold again. Her fourth owner was a Turkish general who bought her for his cruel wife and mother-in-law. In her biography, she related that if anyone was even a minute late, the wife would beat the person with a whip. If a slave got sick, they were left to die, and their body was tossed on the manure heap.

Khartoum, the sixth-largest metropolitan area in Africa, is the capital of Sudan. It is located where the White Nile and the Blue Nile come together to flow to the Mediterranean. The origin of the name of the city is uncertain, but some scholars think it may derive from the name of the Egyptian creator god, Atum, since Sudan or Kush as it is known in the Bible was the home of the black Pharaohs.

• •

Josephine and another young girl almost managed to escape the first slavers. When they were briefly left unchained, they ran into the forest and spent the night in a tree to avoid wild animals, most likely lions, that were stalking them. They were found by a man they initially believed was rescuing them, but who then resold them to the slavers.

The cruelest punishment Bakhita endured during this period was scarification. She says that her mistress wanted her and some other slaves marked in a process that involved drawing patterns on the breast, belly, and right arm, then cutting deeply into the skin and rubbing salt into the wounds to ensure permanent scarring. Josephine had 114 such cuts made and later said "that the reason I did not die was the Lord miraculously destined me for better things."

Josephine's fortune improved somewhat when her master had to return to Turkey and was forced to sell his slaves. In 1883, she was purchased by the Italian Consul in Khartoum, Callisto Legnani, who treated her kindly. When the Consul was called back to Italy, he and a friend, Augusto Michieli, planned to travel together. Josephine asked to accompany them. Upon arrival in Italy, the Consul gave Josephine to Michieli's wife, Turina, and she became the nanny to their daughter Alice, known as Mimmina. After three years, Michieli and his family returned to Suakin, Sudan, where he had a hotel.

Josephine worked in the hotel bar and canteen shop. After nine months, Michieli's wife and daughter returned to Italy with plans to sell their Italian properties and move permanently to Africa. When the real estate dealings took longer than expected, Mrs. Michieli wanted to visit her husband, so she left her daughter and Josephine in the care of the Canossian Sisters in Venice. This changed everything for Josephine.

Despite undergoing horrendous torture, Josephine was never sexually abused by her owners. When asked about this by her superior, she said, "I have been in the middle of mud, but I never got dirty."

• • • • • • • • • • • • • • • • • • • •

Numerous ethnic groups in Africa traditionally practiced scarification primarily as a rite of passage such as entering puberty or marriage. It was also used to help with tribal identification as well as for beautification. While scarification still occurs, tattooing has become increasingly more popular because of the decreased risk of major infection.

• • • • • • • • • • • • • • • • • • • •

Suakin is a port city on the Red Sea in northeastern Sudan. At one time, it was a luxurious destination, thought to be Ptolemy's Port of Good Hope. In 2018, Turkey was granted a 99-year lease over the area. Turkey has plans to rebuild a ruined Ottoman city on the site.

The Canossians trace their origin to St. Magdalen of Canossa. Magdalen founded the Canossian Daughters of Charity in Verona, Italy, in 1809, primarily as a missionary order. Today they are in thirty-two countries working in education, catechesis, and care for the sick. Magdalen was declared a saint in 1988.

At the Canossian convent, Josephine, who had been forced to become a Muslim by her early owners, began to learn about Catholicism. She wrote, "Those holy mothers instructed me with heroic patience and introduced me to that God who from childhood I had felt in my heart without knowing who He was." When Mrs. Michieli came back from Sudan to collect her daughter and Josephine, Josephine refused to go. She said that while she loved Mrs. Michieli and Alice, she could not "lose God" by returning to Africa. Mrs. Michieli did all she could to force the issue, but Josephine wouldn't budge. Finally, on November 29, 1889, an Italian court ruled that because Italian law did not recognize slavery, Bakhita was no longer a slave. Choosing to remain with the Canossian Sisters, she was baptized Josephine Margaret Fortunata on January 9, 1890. "Fortunata" is the Latin translation of Bahkita.

In December of 1893, she entered the novitiate of the Canossian Sisters and took her vows three years later. In 1902, she was assigned to a convent in Vicenza, located forty miles west of Venice, where she spent the rest of her life, except for a few years when, based out of Milan, she traveled and spoke of her experiences as a slave at other Canossian convents.

Most of her life, she worked as a cook, sacristan, and doorkeeper. Even though she was in a great deal of pain in her last years, when asked how she was, she would always say, "As the Master desires." In her final hours, she thought she was back in slavery and cried out, "The chains are too tight, loosen them a little, please."

She died on February 8, 1947, and was canonized in October 2000. Her feast day is February 8, and she is the patron saint of Sudan and victims of human trafficking.

Legends, Lore, and Miracles

When Josephine was telling her story to a nun who was writing her biography, she said that during the night when she and the other slave girl who had escaped with her were hiding in the forest, she saw a beautiful figure of light who pointed the way to escape the wild beasts. Many years later, she saw the same figure of light in the rectory. She said that she came to believe the figure was her Guardian Angel. She is said to have developed such a close relationship with her angel that when she was bedridden and couldn't get to Mass, she said, "Do not worry. I send my guardian angel so that he will tell me about it later."

When Pope John Paul II visited Sudan in February 1993 he said, "Rejoice, all of Africa! Bakhita has come back to you. The daughter of Sudan sold into slavery as a living piece of merchandise and yet still free. Free with the freedom of the saints."

In his encyclical *Spe Salvi* (In Hope We Were Saved) Pope Benedict XVI told Josephine's life story.

Two of the miracles associated with Josephine involve cures. In the first, in October 1947, a young nun faced drastic knee surgery because of a severe infection. Before the surgery, she and two other nuns prayed a novena to Josephine, who had died the previous February. The night before the operation, a voice was heard telling the young nun to "Get up, wake up and walk." The next day, the doctors could find no trace of disease in her knee.

In a second case, in 1976, a Brazilian woman who suffered from diabetic ulcers faced amputation of her legs. The woman prayed, "Bakhita, you who suffered so much, please help me, heal my legs!" By the next day, she was completely healed.

Quote

"If I were to meet those who kidnapped me, and even those who tortured me, I would kneel and kiss their hands. For, if these things had not happened, I would not have been a Christian and a religious today."

Recipe

—————◆◆◆◆—————

Moukhbaza-Inspired Banana and Chili Fritters with Chili-Cardamom Sugar

Moukhbaza is a traditional Sudanese dish made with mashed banana paste, topped with a spicy green pepper sauce, then drizzled with olive oil. The components of this dish are transformed into delightful spicy-sweet fritters.

- **PREP TIME:** 15 minutes
- **COOK TIME:** 10-15 minutes
- **YIELD:** About 18 fritters
- **SPECIAL EQUIPMENT:** Helpful – candy thermometer to gauge oil temperature and small scoop for batter.
- **THIS RECIPE IS LACTO-OVO VEGETARIAN.** It contains milk and egg.

INGREDIENTS

2 tablespoons fresh serrano chili
   (or your favorite fresh spicy pepper)
   seeds and stem removed, finely chopped
3 tablespoons olive oil
2 ripe bananas, peeled
1 teaspoon lemon juice
1 cup plus 2 tablespoons flour
¼ cup packed brown sugar
1 tablespoon baking powder
2 teaspoons baking soda
⅛ teaspoon ground cayenne pepper
¼ teaspoon ground coriander
¼ teaspoon cardamom
1 teaspoon cinnamon
¼ teaspoon ground red pepper (dried)

½ teaspoon salt
½ cup milk
1 egg
Oil for deep-frying with high smoke
   point, such as canola, sunflower,
   or safflower oils.

Chili-Cardamom Sugar for Coating
⅓ cup sugar
½ teaspoon cardamom
1 teaspoon cinnamon
¼ teaspoon ground cayenne pepper
   (dried)
   Pinch of salt

DIRECTIONS

- Sauté the chilis in olive oil over medium-low heat for 5 minutes until softened. Set aside to cool.
- In medium bowl, mash the bananas with lemon juice. Add the chili/olive oil mixture and stir.
- In a separate bowl, combine the dry ingredients (flour, brown sugar, baking powder, baking soda, spices, and salt).
- Add the milk and egg to the banana mixture, mix well. Add the dry ingredients and mix lightly until just combined. The batter should be thick. You may refrigerate up to one hour before deep-frying.

Notes about deep-frying safely:

- Take proper precautions for working with very hot oil. Do not fill pan more than halfway with oil. You only need to deep-fry these in about 5 or so inches of oil. Heat oil slowly and watch for smoking oil. Overheated oil can be flammable. Do not let the oil reach the smoking point. If the oil begins to smoke, turn off the heat and take it off the heat immediately. Always have nearby a baking sheet or metal lid to cover the pot in the event of fire, as well as salt and baking soda. If fire does occur, cover the pot immediately with a baking pan or pot lid, turn off heat source and call 911. Use salt or baking soda to extinguish flames if necessary. Never use water to extinguish an oil fire. As soon as you have finished deep-frying, turn off heat and carefully move the pot off heat source to a non-heated area on stovetop.

- Heat cooking oil in a large high-sided heavy frying pan or pot over medium heat until it reaches 360 degrees on a candy thermometer. If you don't have a thermometer, you may test the oil for readiness by placing a tiny bit of batter in the oil. If it immediately starts to bubble around the batter, the oil is ready.
- Using a small scoop (or a teaspoon and another spoon to push batter into oil), carefully scoop batter into oil, close enough to oil so as not to cause a splash. Do not overcrowd. You will need to work in at least two batches, depending on the size of your pot or pan. Allow to brown well on one side, then flip the fritter using metal tongs or a metal slotted spoon. Total deep-fry time is about 4 minutes. Test one fritter before removing them all from the oil: Remove one fritter and cut open at once to ensure batter is cooked through. If not, extend the frying time and test one fritter again. Remove from oil when browned and cooked. Turn off heat. Drain on paper towels. Immediately roll in Chili-Cardamom Sugar and serve warm.

Prayers

TRADITIONAL PRAYER

St. Josephine Bakhita, you were sold into slavery as a child and endured untold hardship and suffering. Once liberated from your physical enslavement, you found true redemption in your encounter with Christ and his Church. O St. Bakhita, assist all those who are trapped in a state of slavery; intercede with God on their behalf so that they will be released from their chains of captivity. Those whom man enslaves, let God set free. Provide comfort to survivors of slavery and let them look to you as an example of hope and faith. Help all survivors find healing from their wounds. We ask for your prayers and intercessions for those enslaved among us. Amen. [2]

CONTEMPORARY PRAYER

St. Josephine, help us to forgive those who have trespassed against us and to always see ourselves being "fortunate" to be loved by God. Amen.

CHAPTER 10
St. Francis Borgia

On his way out of the kitchen, where Martha assured him she would take care of his pasta, Francis Borgia paused at the appetizers and cautiously sampled one salty locust. As he walked the length of the buffet table, he looked around quickly and discretely spat it into a napkin.

"Not fond of locusts?" Francis of Assisi chuckled as they met at the desserts.

"I didn't think anyone had seen," Borgia said sheepishly.

"You're braver than I am," Francis said. "Eating locusts sounds like penance. Actually, it sounds like more than penance." He gave a little shudder. "Bugs," he said, "At least John the Baptist didn't eat spiders or we'd be looking at a dish of them."

> The Borgias were an Italian-Spanish noble family who became important in both church and civic affairs during the fifteenth and sixteenth centuries. St. Francis Borgia was the grandson of the notorious Rodrigo Borgia, better known as Pope Alexander VI.

"That would be a bit much," Borgia agreed. "I hope he didn't see me spitting out his treat." Borgia looked around the room a bit nervously.

"I don't think so," Francis said. "He seems to be talking with Martin and Gertrude."

Borgia let his shoulders relax a bit. "I am grateful that we no longer have to perform penances," said. "They certainly serve their purpose on earth, discipline and all that, but I have to admit I don't miss them."

"Nor do I," Francis agreed.

Borgia went on, "As I've had time to reflect, I think I may have gone a wee bit overboard in the penance department."

"You and I both," Francis said. "I used to think that I had to perform the most severe penances in order to follow the example of Christ." He gave a little self-deprecating snort. "Once someone told me that I looked like a living corpse. I'll admit that I was quite strict about fasting. One Lent I ate only a half a loaf of bread the entire time. That was probably a bit much."

"Pulse" refers to members of the legume family like peas and beans. The children's rhyme "Peas porridge hot" describes how during the Middle Ages, a thick porridge would be kept over the fire, with whatever new vegetables that could be found added to it. Because the pot was never completely emptied, it could well be "nine days old" at some point.

• •

Borgia was so heavy at one point that he had to have a half circle cut in the dining table so that he could sit comfortably. After entering religious life, he became so thin, it was said he could fold his excess skin around him like a robe.

Borgia nodded in solemn agreement. "You and I had more in common than our name," he said. "I used to eat only one meal a day of leeks, pulse porridge, bread, and water. I would have fasted as strenuously as you did, but I had all kinds of noble guests coming to dinner, and I tried not to call too much attention to myself. I would eat my leek and porridge as slowly as I could so that no one noticed I wasn't eating anything else."

"My intentions were good," Borgia went on. "I had been quite overweight before becoming a Jesuit, but I might have taken fasting too far. I think I could have been a better Vicar-General of the Jesuits if I hadn't had so many digestive issues as a result of an extreme diet. Doctors later told me that my overall health had been affected."

"My dear brother, I fully understand," Francis said. "If I had it to do over, I might have been gentler on myself. My body—I used to call it Brother Ass—took more punishment than was needed. I have to admit I sinned against it."

Borgia seemed to gaze into his past. "I used to flagellate myself, up to 800 strokes a day. And I wore an iron girdle."

"And I regularly used a whip," Francis said.

The two Francises stood in silence for a moment. "I think it's a good thing that such severe penances are no longer in vogue on earth," Borgia said. "I've come to realize that God loves us, not for what we do to ourselves, but for how much we have loved. But," he added with a slight chuckle, "I might suggest to a few moderns that wearing sackcloth or hair shirts wouldn't be entirely out of the question."

"Isn't it funny how people are willing to wear uncomfortable things, like high heels and corsets, for fashion but not for penance?" Francis said. "It's like modern dieting, don't you think? People are willing to eat almost nothing to lose weight, but fasting for religious purposes seems too hard. But we did our best with what we knew at the time, right?"

"Indeed," Borgia agreed. "That's all anyone can do."

Francis agreed. "Even saints. I've always wondered something," he said, suddenly changing the topic. "I hope you don't find me rude, but what was it like being the 'white sheep' of the Borgia clan? I heard stories from some of the Jesuits up here. It seems your relatives were quite something!"

A hairshirt or cilice is an undergarment made of coarse animal hair. It is quite uncomfortable and is worn as a means of self-mortification and penance. As far as penances go, wearing a hairshirt is one of the less stringent since it doesn't cause bodily harm like flagellation. St. Ignatius Loyola, St. Padre Pio, and Pope Paul VI are known to have worn cilices. Wearing sackcloth, which is somewhat like burlap, is a similar penance.

• •

The Borgia family tree can be confusing; Pope Alexander VI had four children with his mistress Vannozza Gattenei. One of their sons, Juan, was married to Maria Enrique de Luna. They had a son, also named Juan, whose son was St. Francis Borgia. Through their finagling and intrigue, two Borgias became popes: Pope Callixtus III (1455–1458) and Pope Alexander VI (1492–1503). The entire Borgia clan was known for sexual immorality including incest, as well as theft, bribery, simony, and murder, especially through the use of poison.

Borgia laughed, a deep rumbling laugh at odds with his lean, drawn face. "No one wanted to go to one of Lucrezia's dinner parties, that's for sure." He remembered finding a ring in a box and picking it up when he was a little boy. His mother swooped in and grabbed it from him. "That was Lucrezia's," she almost shouted. "It's probably got poison it in." Borgia had been slightly suspicious of all jewelry, especially rings, ever since then. When his wife wore jewelry for a state dinner, he always preferred that she choose necklaces over rings.

Lucrezia was the daughter of Pope Alexander and his mistress. Her family arranged several marriages for her that advanced the fame and fortune of the Borgias. Praised as a beauty in her time, she was also an intelligent and level-headed administrator. In fact, she was the Governor of Spoleto, a position usually headed by a cardinal. As a result of her marriages and affairs, she had numerous complicated pregnancies and miscarriages. She died as a result of childbirth from her tenth child. Lucrezia was said to have been a notorious poisoner, often concealing the poison in a special ring.

• •

The Poor Clares are a contemplative order of nuns founded by Clare of Assisi and Francis of Assisi on Palm Sunday 1212. The daughter of a well-to-do family, Clare ran away to join Francis. At first, she lived in a Benedictine monastery, but eventually, with the aid of Francis, she, her mother, two of her sisters, and some other women set up their own convent in 1216. The Eternal Word Television Network (EWTN) is operated by the Poor Clares of Perpetual Adoration in Birmingham, Alabama.

"When you have relatives like Pope Alexander and Lucrezia, it isn't all that hard to be better behaved," he chuckled. "All it would have taken to be a 'white sheep' was to have been a moderately decent person." He suddenly grew serious. "We don't get to choose our family, my friend. And we don't always get to choose the course of our lives. You, of all people, must know this."

Francis nodded. "All too well."

Borgia templed his fingers. "I learned at a very young age that along with evil, one can always find some good. It's just that the good sometimes comes in mysterious ways. When my grandfather married Grandmother Maria Enrique de Luna, everything changed."

"Ah yes. Your grandmother was under the influence of the Poor Clares. I get credit for the Franciscans, but Clare was a force unto herself. Her sisters were—well, still are—something else," Francis said.

"I think it was because of my grandmother that I wanted to be a monk from the time I was a child, but becoming a duke came first. I was happy as a married man," Borgia said. "But I always felt that God was calling me to something else. I was twice blessed, to have a family and yet to live out a religious calling. But enough about the past. Do you know when the party is supposed to start? I don't mind eating cold pasta, but it's much better when it's hot."

"I think we are all here," Francis said, quickly counting heads. "So it can't be too much longer before the honored guest arrives." He looked expectantly at the entrance.

"Do you really think they will come in through the front door?" Borgia asked. "I think it's more likely we should keep an eye on the kitchen door."

Francis laughed. "You know, you're probably right. Or not through any door at all, but just appear."

Borgia nodded, and a wry smile brightened his otherwise somber expression.

Did You Know?

St. Francis Borgia was St. Teresa of Avila's confessor.

⇥ BIOGRAPHY

St. Francis Borgia

OCTOBER 28, 1510 – SEPTEMBER 30, 1572

F rancis Borgia would have been a noted historical figure even if he weren't a saint. The great-grandson of a corrupt pope, he was a Spanish aristocrat, and eventually the third Superior General of the Jesuits, not to mention being a loving husband and father and the fourth Duke of Gandia.

Modern Gandia is located on the Mediterranean in eastern Spain forty miles south of Valencia. Once a Greek settlement, Gandia was taken over by the Moors in the eighth century. It was recaptured by James I of Aragon in 1252 and became a duchy of the Borgia family.

• •

Borgia was only nineteen when he married. This was not as young as it would seem to us. At that time, people often married in the late teens and were considered adults by the age of sixteen or so. Girls, in particular, were often married by age twelve or thirteen.

Under the influence of his pious grandmother, who herself was influenced by the Poor Clares, Francis desired to become a monk, but at age seventeen, was sent to the court of the Holy Roman Emperor Charles V. A bright and engaging young man, he soon distinguished himself and accompanied the emperor on many occasions. One of the most notable excursions was to transport the corpse of Isabella of Portugal to her final burial spot. By the time they arrived, the body was so badly decomposed that people could barely stand to be in the same room. This deeply affected Francis and is said to have greatly influenced his later desire to renounce his fortune.

In the meantime, in 1529, he married Eleanora de Castro Mello y Meneses, with whom he had eight children, and, in 1543, he became the fourth Duke of Gandia.

By all accounts, he and his wife had a happy marriage. They were devout in their religious duties, but equally dedicated to each other and their children. When Eleanora died after a difficult illness, Francis decided to renounce his titles in order to enter religious life. However, being a devoted father, he put off his desire until his children were old enough to do without him as a hands-on-parent. He was aided in this by his wife's sister, who took on many of the duties of being a mother. Five years after Eleanora's death, he handed over his titles to his eldest son, Charles, and was ordained as a Jesuit priest.

Because of his administrative abilities, he soon assumed leadership roles, including being responsible for all the missions in the East and West Indies. His skills led him to become noticed by Pope Julius III, who wanted to make him a cardinal, an honor Francis did not want and was ultimately able to avoid.

In 1565, he became the third Superior General of Jesuits. Among his many accomplishments was to help fund the founding of the Gregorian University in Rome, something he had longed to do since his first visit to Rome. Under his leadership, the Jesuits spread the gospel all over the world.

In 1572, Pope Pius V asked him to embark on a diplomatic mission to the court of France. The journey proved to be too much for Francis, and his health took a precipitous downturn. Wishing to die in Rome, he was eventually taken on a litter to the Eternal City. On this final journey, people came out from all the villages along the route saying, "We wish to see the saint." Through sheer grit, he lived long enough to die in his own room on September 30. His feast day is October 10, the day closest to his death that was not already taken by another saint. He is remembered as a patron against earthquakes.

Today the Pontifical Gregorian University has about 2,700 students from around the world. Its programs include theology, canon law, philosophy, and Church history, among others. One-third of the current members of the College of Cardinals have studied there, and more than 900 bishops are listed among its alumni.

Legends, Lore, and Miracles

While serving the court of Charles V, he once passed a man being led to prison by the Inquisition. That man was St. Ignatius of Loyola.

It is said that so many people attended his first Mass, it had to be held outdoors.

The only time he is remembered as becoming angry was when someone would treat him as if he were still a duke, calling him "my lord" and "your grace."

One legend surrounding the saint claims that a "heretic" once said, "Upon my word, you seem to make very sure that this famous Duke of Gandia is in Heaven, in spite of all his absurd superstitions and imaginary miracles! Rather than believe that he is in reality gone there, I call upon God to send me down to Hell this very moment, body and soul." No sooner had he said these words, than the earth opened up under him and he disappeared.

One of the most famous miracle stories attributed to Francis Borgia involved a young woman named Apollonia Cavalli, who, in a misguided attempt to emulate the sufferings of Christ, burned her breast with a red-hot iron and then put a blistering powder into the wound. When infection became severe, she had to see a doctor, who told her there was nothing he could do. She went to her confessor, who gave her a small picture and a relic of St. Francis. She went home, and that night St. Francis is said to have appeared to her in a dream, telling her that she was cured. When she awoke, all that remained was a large scar.

While he could not completely avoid the principal pastimes of the upper class, which included hawking while he was duke, Francis was said to have closed his eyes at the moment his hawk swooped, thus avoiding seeing the actual kill.

Quote

"We must make our way towards eternity,
never regarding what men think of us or our actions,
studying only to please God."

Recipe

———◦◇◦———

Pesto Pasta with Roasted Cippolini Onions and Vegetables

Although Francis himself ate very modestly (in later life), he always made sure that he served his guests well-prepared and ample meals. This dish is reflective of Francis's adopted home of Rome.

- **PREP TIME**: Roasted vegetables: 25 minutes / Pesto 10 minutes
- **COOK TIME**: Roasted vegetables: 25 minutes / Pasta Boil Time: Varies.
- **SERVES**: 8
- **SPECIAL EQUIPMENT**: Food processor or blender for pesto.
- **MAKE IT VEGAN** by substituting with your favorite vegan Parmesan-style cheese. Substitute butter with additional olive oil. Use vegan (egg-free) pasta.
- **MAKE IT GLUTEN-FREE** by using gluten-free pasta and gluten-free grated hard cheese.

INGREDIENTS

1 pound cippolini onions	2 tablespoons butter
1 bunch (about 14 oz.) fresh asparagus	1 tablespoon olive oil
3 bell peppers (one yellow, one red, one green)	2 cloves garlic, finely chopped
	Sea salt
2 yellow squash	Ground black pepper
1 zucchini	1 pound pasta of your choice, cooked

DIRECTIONS

- Preheat oven to 400 degrees Fahrenheit.
- De-skin the Cipollini onions: Drop onions in a pot of boiling water for 90 seconds. Drain and immediately put onions in ice water to cool. In order to leave the onions whole and intact, trim just a bit off the root. If you cut the entire root end off, the onions may fall apart. Remove skins by pulling off with paring knife.
- Rinse asparagus under cold water. Hold an asparagus stalk by the very ends with each hand. Start bending the stalk until it breaks naturally above the thicker (stem) end. Discard stems.
- Rinse the bell peppers, cut in half lengthwise. Discard seeds and remove stem portion. Remove white pith. Cut peppers into strips, lengthwise.

- Rinse squash and zucchini under cold water. Cut off the stem and the very tip of the other end. Cut squash and zucchini diagonally: Make the first cut at a 45-degree angle on stem end. Proceed cutting ¾" slices following this angle. If you'd rather, simply slice each into circles ¾" thick.
- Place roasting pan in preheated oven for a few minutes. Remove pan from oven and place butter and olive oil in pan and allow butter to melt. Add onions, sprinkle with pinch of sea salt and black pepper. Toss to coat onions. Roast for 7 minutes, stir. Roast for 7 more minutes. Add asparagus, peppers, squash, zucchini, and garlic to roasting pan. Add pinch more of sea salt and black pepper. Add additional drizzle of olive oil if needed. Stir. Roast 10 minutes. Stir. Roast additional 4–5 minutes until all vegetables are cooked.

INGREDIENTS FOR THE PESTO

2 oz. pine nuts
½ cup almonds, blanched and skinless
   (whole, slivered or sliced)
3½ ounces fresh basil leaves
¼-½ cup extra virgin olive oil

3 cloves fresh garlic
¾ cup Parmigiano-Reggiano,
   or similar grated cheese,
   plus additional to top dish
Salt and pepper to taste

DIRECTIONS FOR THE PESTO

- Place the pine nuts and almonds in a dry sauté pan over medium heat to toast until lightly browned, stirring occasionally. Cool. Place pine nuts and almonds in in food processor with steel blade. Process for 15 seconds. Add basil, cheese, and garlic. Process for 15 seconds, then drizzle in olive oil while processing. Only add enough olive oil until pesto is a thick, creamy consistency. Add salt and pepper to taste.
- Serve with your choice of pasta cooked according to directions. After draining the pasta, return it to cooking pot. Add pesto. Over low heat: Gently stir to distribute pesto onto pasta. Heat for a few minutes. Turn out Pesto Pasta into a large serving bowl. Top with roasted vegetables. Sprinkle with grated cheese.

Prayers

TRADITIONAL PRAYER

How precious is this prerogative in thy case, O Francis, for it concerns the virtue which attracts God's grace in this life, and wins such glory hereafter! Since pride has hurled Lucifer into the abyss, and the self-abasement of the Son of God has led to His exaltation above the heavens—humility, whatever men may now say, has lost nothing of its inestimable value; it is still the indispensable foundation of every durable edifice, whether spiritual or social; the basis, without which the other virtues, and even charity the Queen of them all, could not subsist a single day. Therefore, O Francis, obtain for us this humility; thoroughly convince us of the vanity of this world's honors and false pleasures. May the holy Society, which thou after St. Ignatius didst render still more valuable to the Church, cherish this spirit of thine, so that it may deserve more and more the esteem of heaven and the gratitude of earth. Amen.

CONTEMPORARY PRAYER

St. Francis, you know what it is like to go from one extreme to another in life. Help me to have the wisdom to find balance in all things so that I might carry out the duties of my state of life in health and joy. Amen.

CHAPTER 11

St. Francis of Assisi

$\mathcal{S}$ uddenly the kitchen door cracked open and both Francises looked expectantly, but when they realized it was only Martha checking on the buffet table, they relaxed again.

"You called me the 'white sheep' of the Borgias," Francis Borgia said, "but what about you? What do you think of yourself?"

Francis of Assisi tugged his little beard. "That's an interesting question. I suspect my family might have thought that I was a 'black sheep' since I didn't go into the family business, and I actually caused them quite a bit of embarrassment when I walked around town dressed in, well, let's just say, not always the cleanest of clothes. And, as much as I hate to have to admit it, I was kind of a jerk at times, especially to my dad."

"But," he added quietly, "The thing that I still think about is that I caused my mother more than her share of heartache." He grew pensive. "Once, my father locked me in a small room because he thought I had gone crazy. When he left on business, my mother let me out. My father was furious when he found out . . . and my mother had to bear the brunt of his anger. She really was a saint for putting up with me."

Once Francis hired a person to follow his father, Pietro di Bernadone around town, drawing crowds and calling out for blessings for Bernadone. His father was not at all pleased by the attention. Another time he took cloth from his father's shop to sell to give the money to the poor. When he didn't think he had made enough money, he sold his father's horse that he had used to carry the cloth!

• •

When Francis was really down and out, his mother used to slip him a little money on the side. She had some money of her own from her dowry, so she did not always have to tell her husband.

"There are things I might have done differently as, I'm sure, so would've you," Borgia said. "As I said before, we do the best we can with what we know at the time."

Although Francis was notoriously hard on himself, he understood the need for compassion for others. One story says that when a friar could not sleep for the pangs of hunger from fasting, Francis brought him some bread and ate some himself to avoid the friar's feeling embarrassed for breaking his fast.

"Very true," Francis of Assisi said. "It's like the mortifications we both undertook. I finally had to apologize to my body. I realized that I had to take care of my body a little better than I had done in the past."

"You know, I sort of envy you," he said suddenly. "I mean, if we could envy up here."

"Why is that?" Borgia asked, his brow creasing in confusion.

Francis sighed. "It's that prayer. The 'Prayer of St. Francis.'"

"You mean the one that begins, 'Lord, make me an instrument of your peace'?"

"That's the one," Francis said with a deep sigh.

"It's a very nice prayer," Borgia said. "People pray it all the time. But what does that have to do with envying me?" he asked, a look of confusion on his face.

"You did just as much as I did, probably more actually," Francis said, "but you don't have people using your name and making up fanciful stories about you all the time and writing things and then putting your name on them. Fame is not what people on earth think it is," he said firmly. "You get recognized for the work you did for the Church. Me? Everyone from environmentalists to prophets thinks they can claim me as one of their own and put words in my mouth. And don't get me started on that *Brother Sun, Sister Moon* movie. Because of that, people think that I was some sort of holy hippie wandering around meadows talking to birds all the time.

The Peace Prayer attributed to Francis first appeared in a French magazine called *La Clochette* (Little Bell) about 1912. No author was named, but many think it was Father Esther Bourquerel, the founder of the League of the Holy Mass. Franciscans point out that the second half does bear some resemblances to the sayings of one of Francis's closest friends and followers, Giles of Assisi. Pope John Paul II recited it at the first World Day of Prayer for Peace in 1986, and Mother Teresa of Calcutta frequently prayed it.

> Lord, make me an instrument of your peace:
> where there is hatred, let me sow love;
> where there is injury, pardon;
> where there is doubt, faith;
> where there is despair, hope;
> where there is darkness, light;
> where there is sadness, joy.
>
> O divine Master, grant that I may not so much seek
> to be consoled as to console,
> to be understood as to understand,
> to be loved as to love.
> For it is in giving that we receive,
> it is in pardoning that we are pardoned,
> and it is in dying that we are born to eternal life.
> Amen.

Brother Sun, Sister Moon is a semi-biographical 1972 Franco Zeffirelli film about the life of St. Francis that was typical of the sentiments of the 1970s.

• • • • • • • • • • • • • • • • •

Jacoba dei Settesoli was a Roman widow who met Francis when he and his followers came to Rome to have the Franciscan Order approved. Francis told her not to leave her family, so she never entered religious life, but she did give some of her property to Francis to use as a hospice. Even though women were not allowed to enter the friary, Francis made an exception for Brother Jacoba, as he fondly called her.

• • • • • • • • • • • • • • • • •

His mother baptized him Giovanni (John) at the time of his birth, but when his father returned from a business trip to France, he renamed him Francesco (Francis)—the Frenchman—either because of his profitable business in France or because of his fondness for all things French.

Francis sighed. "It's not like it's a new thing. People were trying to rewrite my life from the beginning. I kept telling them that I wasn't a saint, and they kept insisting I was. One thing that hasn't made it into most of the stories is that on my deathbed I wanted my close friend Lady Jacoba to visit and bring me almond cookies. Actually, that's what I brought for the potluck." He pointed to a plate filled with sugar-covered cookies. "Somehow a 'saint,'" he said the word with self-deprecation, "wasn't supposed to be visited by a woman and then have the desire for something sweet as a last meal, so that has been glossed over, but she was there with me, and so were the cookies."

Borgia chuckled. "I can see your point. I guess I didn't really appreciate how lucky I've been to be under the 'saint radar' in recent times. On my deathbed, I was visited by my children and grandchildren. The leader of a religious order isn't supposed to have his family with him, now are they?"

"Not in the modern world," Francesco agreed.

Just then, a stately woman placed a steaming dish on the table. "That smells wonderful," Borgia said, drawing a deep breath.

"Bacon," the woman said. "You can't go wrong with bacon. I'm Gertrude, Gertrude of Nivelles," she added. "And you are the two Francises—Borgia and Assisi."

"Guilty as charged," said Francis of Assisi, "but I generally go by Francesco. I suppose I could go by Giovanni since that was my birth name."

"Then Pope Francis would be Pope Giovanni," Gertrude laughed. "He'd be Giovanni XXIV, and we all know that's not going to happen." She turned to Borgia. "I know that the Pope said he took the name 'Francis' after our friend here, but I can't help but think that being a Jesuit, he had you in mind as well."

Borgia had the good grace to blush just a little. "You are too kind," he murmured.

"Now," Gertrude said brusquely. "I need to talk to Francesco about an animal, being the patron of animals and all that."

"What kind of animal?" Francesco asked.

"A cat."

"I don't think I'm the right person," Francis said, shaking his head. "I'm more of a wolf person. I never had pets. If you want to talk about cats, I think you need to see Martin. He is the cat lover."

"So I've been told," Gertrude said.

Did You Know?

Francis had brothers and sisters, although the exact number and names have been lost to history.

⇻ BIOGRAPHY

St. Francis of Assisi

1181 – OCTOBER 3, 1226

Francis was born sometime between 1181 and 1182 to a wealthy Italian cloth and spice merchant, Pietro di Bernardone of Moriconi, and his wife Lady Pica Bourlemont, who was likely from the Provençal region of France. Francis enjoyed the good life afforded to him by his wealthy parents, indulging his fancy for parties and fine clothes. Nevertheless, even early in life, he was said to have a soft heart for beggars, giving them alms when he could. In November 1202, when Francis was twenty, he was overcome by the romance of chivalry and joined the army in a war between Assisi and Perugia. Soon taken prisoner, he spent a year in captivity. That and a severe illness deeply affected him, although upon his recovery, he resumed the life of a wealthy dilettante.

Perugia is a region of Umbria in Italy. For many centuries, it attempted to remain an independent state, going to war with several of its neighbors, including Foligno, Spoleto, Todi, and Assisi. Today the city is famous for its chocolate and hosts a chocolate festival in the fall.

• •

Once, when asked if he was thinking of marrying since he had given up so many of his worldly pleasures, Francis said, "Yes, a fairer bride than any of you have ever seen," which has been interpreted as his desire to "wed" Lady Poverty.

Ever restless, once again, in 1205, Francis decided to reenlist in the army. It was during this period that he reported having the first of many visions. God asked him who it was better to follow: the master or the servant. Francis rightly replied, "The master," and asked God what he should do next. God is said to have told him, "Return to Assisi. This is not your life." Francis did return to Assisi and, to the surprise of his companions, began to change his life.

The next part of Francis's life is a bit less clear. We know that he went to Rome in 1206, where he begged in front of St. Peter's. We also know that it was during this period that he famously met a leper and, overcoming his loathing, kissed the man, whom he came to believe was actually Jesus in disguise. In addition, he took to spending more and more time alone in the countryside outside Assisi. Additionally, we know that at this period his mother was confused by what was happening to her son, and his father was growing increasingly disgruntled. Things got very heated between Francis and his father after Francis had his most famous vision of Jesus in the country chapel of San Damiano outside Assisi. There the icon of the crucified Christ famously said to him, "Francis, Francis, go and repair my house which is falling into ruins."

Francis understood from his vision that he was supposed to literally rebuild the falling-down church, so he took some cloth from his father's shop, sold it, and tried to give the money to the priest at the church. When the priest refused the coin because Francis had stolen the cloth, Francis tossed the money on the ground. Needless to say, when his father learned of the incident, he became furious, and Francis went into hiding for more than a month. When he finally came out, his father had him beaten and locked up in a small room. His mother freed him when her husband was away on a business trip, but when Bernadone

San Damiano is a church with a monastery near Assisi. It was the first convent of the Order of St. Clare. The Romanesque cross, which allegedly spoke to Francis, hangs today in the Basilica of Saint Clare in Assisi. A replica is at San Damiano. Besides Jesus, numerous other figures including the Virgin, St. John, and Mary Magdalene are represented on the cross, as well as some sort of bird, perhaps a rooster.

returned, he decided to be done with his son once and for all. He tried to force Francis to renounce his inheritance, but instead Francis renounced him, saying, "Until now I have called Pietro Bernadone father, but from today I do want to serve only God, so I renounce everything I could inherit from him and I give him back the clothes I wear." Some reports of the incident say Francis stripped completely naked and the bishop who was proceeding over the hearing covered Francis with a cloak.

After this, Francis wandered around the countryside, working for a while at a monastery and rebuilding San Damiano as well as other ruined chapels. It didn't take long for him to attract followers. Soon several men joined him in living a life of radical poverty in dedication to the gospel.

Francis's first followers were Bernardo da Quintavalle, a jurist (an expert on the law), and Pietro Cattani, a law graduate. Next came Egidio, a farmer, as well as Sabatino, Morico, Philip, Longo, Silvestro (a priest), Giovanni della Cappella, Barbaro and Bernardo Vigilante, and Angelo Tancredi. In the crypt at Assisi, along with the tomb of St. Francis, are the tombs of Friar Leo, St. Francis's confessor, and his two other closest friends, Angelo and Rufino.

In July 1209, Pope Innocent III gave him informal permission to found a religious order. The Franciscan order was formally approved by Pope Honorius III in 1223.

Innocent III was reluctant to approve a new order, but he was convinced by a dream he had in which the Basilica of St. John Lateran, the cathedral of the diocese of Rome, was collapsing, except that Francis was there holding it up. The Cathedral of the Most Holy Savior and of Saints John the Baptist and the Evangelist in the Lateran, as it is officially known, is the home church of the Pope as the Bishop of Rome. As such, it ranks superior even to St. Peter's, which is the official church of the Vatican.

Always possessed of an adventurous spirit, Francis tried several times to spread the gospel beyond Italy, but he never succeeded in going very far until 1219, when he traveled to Egypt in an attempt to end the Crusades by converting the Sultan. Francis was not successful, but the Sultan did release him unharmed.

In 1224, during a forty-day fast, he said he had a vision during which he received the stigmata. Brother Leo, who was with him, later wrote, "Suddenly he saw a vision of a seraph, a six-winged angel on a cross. This angel gave him the gift of the five wounds of Christ."

Francis's first biographer, Thomas of Celano, also a Franciscan, wrote in 1230 in the *First Life of St. Francis*:

> His wrists and feet seemed to be pierced by nails, with the heads of the nails appearing on his wrists and on the upper sides of his feet, the points appearing on the other side. The marks were round on the palm of each hand but elongated on the other side, and small pieces of flesh jutting out from the rest took on the appearance of the nail-ends, bent and driven back. In the same way, the marks of nails were impressed on his feet and projected beyond the rest of

the flesh. Moreover, his right side had a large wound as if it had been pierced with a spear, and it often bled so that his tunic and trousers were soaked with his sacred blood.

Francis's health, which was frail from his many penances, gradually began to worsen, and suffering from a painful eye disease and well as possibly malaria, he returned to Assisi, where he died late in the day on October 3, 1226. He was canonized in July 1228 and is celebrated on October 4. He is the patron saint of ecology and animals.

The stigmata are the visible signs of the crucifixion of Jesus. Usually, they appear in the hands, wrists, feet, or head. St. Francis was the first person recorded to have the stigmata. In modern times, St. Padre Pio and St. Mariam Thresia Chiramel of India have been stigmatists.

Legends, Lore, and Miracles

According to legend, Francis was conceived while his parents were on a journey to the Holy Land.

In the *Fioretti* ("Little Flowers"), a collection of stories told soon after Francis's death, one day he and his companions came upon a spot where the trees were filled with birds. Francis told his friends, "Wait for me while I go to preach to my sisters the birds." The birds gathered about him and waited until he had finished his preaching before flying away.

Perhaps the most famous legend told in the *Fioretti* is Francis and the Wolf of Gubbio. Francis lived in Gubbio for a while and realized that a wolf was terrorizing the townspeople. He went out in search of the animal, and when he spotted the beast, Francis made the sign of the cross and said to him:

Brother Wolf, thou hast done much evil in this land, destroying and killing the creatures of God without his permission; yea, not animals only hast thou destroyed, but thou hast even dared to devour men, made after the image of God; for which thing thou art worthy of being hanged like a robber and a murderer. All men cry out against thee, the dogs pursue thee, and all the inhabitants of this city are thy enemies;

but I will make peace between them and thee, O brother wolf, if so
be thou no more offend them, and they shall forgive thee all thy
past offences, and neither men nor dogs shall pursue thee any more.

The wolf submitted to Francis, who continued:

As thou art willing to make this peace, I promise thee that thou
shalt be fed every day by the inhabitants of this land so long as thou
shalt live among them; thou shalt no longer suffer hunger, as it is
hunger which has made thee do so much evil; but if I obtain all this
for thee, thou must promise, on thy side, never again to attack any
animal or any human being; dost thou make this promise?

The wolf gave his word by laying his paw in Francis's hand. The creature
then lived for two more years, being fed by the townspeople. Interestingly, the
skeleton of a large wolf was found under the Gubbio church walls when the
church was refurbished in 1872.

Francis created the first known Nativity scene or *crèche*. Around 1220, he
used real animals to create a living scene so that people could experience the
birth of Christ in a visceral way. Two of his biographers, Thomas of Celano
and Saint Bonaventure, say he used a straw-filled manger with a real ox and
donkey.

Quote

"All that we leave in this world will soon perish,
but the charity and good deeds we have done
will earn a reward from God."

Recipe

Honey-Almond Cookies

So much did St. Francis love almond treats prepared by Blessed Jacoba that he requested them on his deathbed. They are slightly chewy on the inside, with a touch of honey.

- **PREP TIME**: 15 minutes
- **BAKE TIME**: 10-12 minutes
- **YIELD**: Approximately 32 cookies
- **SPECIAL EQUIPMENT**: Stand Mixer or Hand-Held Mixer.
- **THIS RECIPE IS LACTO-OVO VEGETARIAN.** If you do not consume honey, replace with agave syrup or corn syrup. (results may vary)
- **MAKE IT GLUTEN-FREE:** Replace flour with a gluten-free baking flour. Ensure that extracts are gluten-free. As always, make sure all of your ingredients are in fact gluten-free.

INGREDIENTS

½ cup butter, room temperature

¾ cup granulated sugar

1 egg

1½ tablespoons honey

1 teaspoon almond extract

½ teaspoon vanilla extract

½ teaspoon lemon juice

1½ cups almond flour

½ cup + 2 tablespoons all-purpose flour

¼ teaspoon salt

Confectioner's sugar for sprinkling over baked cookies, about ¼ cup

DIRECTIONS

Preheat oven to 350 degrees.

- Line two cookie sheets with parchment paper (or spray with non-stick cooking spray, or grease with butter or oil).
- In a mixing bowl, cream the butter and sugar for 3 minutes using an electric or hand mixer. Scrape down sides of bowl with spatula.
- Add the egg, honey, almond extract, vanilla extract, and lemon juice. Mix on high speed for 3 minutes. Scrape down sides of bowl with spatula.
- Mix almond flour, all-purpose flour, and salt in small bowl. Add to creamed butter mixture; mix on low speed until just combined.
- Scoop out a tablespoon at a time (or use a small scoop) onto cookie sheet, spaced 2" apart.
- Bake 10-12 minutes on center rack of oven. When done, they will be light golden on top and lightly browned around edges. Remove from oven and let rest on racks a few minutes. Sprinkle with confectioner's sugar. Transfer to cooling racks.

Prayers

TRADITIONAL PRAYER

You are holy, Lord,
the only God,
and your deeds are wonderful.
You are strong,
you are great,
you are the Most High,
you are the almighty King.
You, holy Father, are King of the heaven
and earth.
You are Three and One,
God above all gods.
You are good, all good, supreme good,
Lord God, living and true.
You are love,
You are wisdom,
You are humility,
You are endurance,
You are beauty,
You are gentleness,
You are security,
You are rest,
You are joy.

You are our hope and happiness,
You are justice and moderation,
You are all our riches,
You are beauty,
You are gentleness,
You are our protector,
You are our guardian
and defender.
You are strength,
You are consolation,
You are our hope,
You are our faith,
You are our charity,
You are all our sweetness,
You are our eternal life,
great and admirable Lord,
God almighty,
merciful Savior.

CONTEMPORARY PRAYER

St. Francis, may your example of whole-hearted dedication to the Lord inspire me to not hold back, not to try to protect my heart, but to love without counting the cost. Amen.

CHAPTER 12

St. Andrew Kim Taegon

Andrew Kim Taegon thought he might have been late since the dining room was full when he arrived, but Solanus assured him that the guest of honor hadn't yet arrived. With great relief, Kim set his kimchi on the buffet table.

He didn't recognize many of the other dishes. *No rice*, he thought. *But the bread and fish look good.* He wandered to the head of the table where he spied a bowl of what looked like fried grasshoppers. He tentatively picked up one and bit down. It gave a satisfying crunch, and he scooped a few more into his hand.

"Do you like them?" John the Baptist came up behind him. "I made them. They're salted locusts."

"Oh, yes," Kim said. "In Asia we eat many different kinds of bugs. They are a very good source of protein," he added.

"Exactly!" John agreed enthusiastically. "I used to eat them while I was in the desert. Sometimes I would cook them with honey for a treat. Unfortunately, not many people here appreciate the finer qualities of entomophagy," he added sadly. "I guess it's an acquired taste."

"I was thinking that perhaps my kimchi might be an acquired taste as well," Kim said.

"Well, as long as it's vegetarian, I'll try it," John said, looking around. "I'm assuming that the guest of honor will be here soon. I'm getting a little hungry."

More than a quarter of the world regularly eats insects. More than 2,100 species are edible, with the most popular being beetles and caterpillars. For their size, insects are extremely nutritious. They are at least comparable per ounce to beef, chicken, and pork in their amounts of protein, omega-3 fats, iron, magnesium, calcium, and zinc.

• •

Kimchi dates back to approximately 37 BC, although fermented foods like kimchi have been eaten for millennia because fermentation is a very safe means of preserving food for long periods. In Korea, kimchi was often buried in the ground in ceramic pots called *onggi* to last the winter. Radish kimchi was especially popular in the Goryeo dynasty, which lasted from 918–1392.

"Perhaps you should have a few more locusts," Kim said with a smile, pointing to the dish. John reached out and put a few in his hand. "By the way, I'm very glad to see you here," Kim continued. "I've been meaning to talk to you about Andrew."

"Andrew?"

"Yes, the Apostle Andrew, my namesake. He was one of your disciples, wasn't he?" John nodded, his mouth full of locusts. "I admired him for his zeal in accepting Jesus as the Messiah," Kim continued.

John swallowed before continuing, "That is the most notable thing about him. I was impressed with how quickly he recognized Jesus as the Lord. People sometimes think that Peter was the first apostle, but it was Andrew. If Andrew hadn't introduced Jesus to Peter, history would have been very different."

The Gospel of John says that John was walking with Andrew and another unnamed disciple when John saw Jesus and said, "Look, the Lamb of God." When the disciples heard this, they spent the rest of the day with Jesus. Immediately after that, Andrew went to his brother Peter and said, "We have found the Messiah," and took Peter to meet Jesus.

• •

A Korean girl, Julia Ota-a, was captured by a Japanese commander named Konishi Yukinaga and taken to Japan, where she became one of the first Koreans to convert to Christianity. Portuguese Catholics had arrived in Japan as early as 1549. It was difficult to send missionaries to Korea because the government refused all contact with the outside world except to pay annual taxes to China. The first French missionaries did not arrive until 1836.

Kim looked pensive. "History often turns on what seems like a small thing, doesn't it? A few right—or wrong words. I don't mean to be impolite, but if Herod hadn't asked Salome what she wanted as a reward, you might not have, well, you know." He looked away so as not to embarrass either of them. "Do you know the history of Christianity in Korea?" Kim asked, in an effort to quickly change the subject from beheading, John's or his own.

"I can't say that I do," John admitted.

"Christianity came about 1592 when the Japanese invaded our country," Kim explained.

"About a year later, a Jesuit priest visited, and not long after that, a Korean diplomat brought to my country several books about Christianity written by a Jesuit missionary to China. That is how it all began: with the power of the written word. When a Chinese priest secretly entered Korea a dozen or so years later, there were 4,000 Christians. None of them had ever seen a priest!" Kim said in admiration. "Seven years later, there were 10,000 Christians. One thing that really helped Christianity take off was when people began to embrace the idea that merit counted more than where you were born in the social strata." Kim looked down. "I am sorry to have become so pedantic. I was accustomed to giving sermons when I was on earth and I am still doing it here. My apologies."

"Never apologize," John said emphatically. "Your sermons converted hundreds. And I am always happy to learn about a part of the world I never visited in my earthly lifetime."

Just then, Solanus Casey walked up. "What are you two talking about?" he asked. "Theology?"

Kim shook his head bemusedly. "History. The history of Christianity in Korea."

"Ah, history. I was never a very good student," Solanus said, "but I enjoyed history."

"Most of what I knew about history came from the Scriptures and that was pretty much just focused on Israel," John added.

"And now you are an important part of history *and* Scripture," Kim teased.

"John, I know you only drink water, but can I get you some wine or beer, Kim?" Solanus asked.

"Do you think there is any soju?" Kim asked.

"I don't know, but I'm sure we can find you some," Solanus said, as he walked toward the wine bar, followed dutifully by Kim.

> Soju, the national liquor of Korea, is traditionally made from rice, wheat, or barley. The name soju means "burned liquor."

Did You Know?

Andrew Kim and his father, Ignatius Kim, were beatified together on July 25, 1925.

≫ BIOGRAPHY

St. Andrew Kim Taegon

AUGUST 21, 1821 – SEPTEMBER 16, 1846

The first Korean-born Catholic priest and martyr, Andrew Kim Taegon was born in central South Korea to Christian converts. His great-grandfather, grand-uncle, and father were martyred during the persecutions of the Joseon Dynasty.

The Joseon Dynasty was founded in 1392 and lasted nearly five centuries until it was replaced by the Korean Empire in 1897. During its height, neo-Confucianism became the state religion. Much of the culture of modern Korea derives from practices founded in the Joseon Dynasty.

Andrew's father, Ignatius Kim, was betrayed by one of his sons-in-law for allowing Andrew to go abroad to study, which was against Korean law, as well as for being a Christian. Under torture, Ignatius denied his Christian faith, but eventually recanted his denial and was beheaded with eight other Catholics in 1839 when his son was eighteen.

After Andrew's baptism at age fifteen, he traveled more than 1,200 miles to study at seminary in the Portuguese colony of Macau. He also studied in the Philippines. He eventually returned to Korea on foot by way of Manchuria, and then, in 1845, he crossed the Yellow Sea to Shanghai, where he was ordained by French bishop Jean Ferréol.

Returning to his native Korea, he was arrested in June of 1846 by the border patrol while trying to smuggle in other missionaries along the southeast coast. On September 26, when he was twenty-five, he was tortured and beheaded near Seoul on the Han River for the crime of being a Christian. Before he was killed, his face was covered with lime and his ears were pierced with arrows.

Kim, along with St. Paul Chong Hasang, ninety-eight other Koreans, and three French missionaries, were canonized on May 6, 1984. Most of the martyrs were laity: forty-seven women and forty-five men. They are commemorated as a group on September 20.

Legends, Lore, and Miracles

We do not have records, yet, of miracles attributed to Andrew Kim Taegon, but because he died a martyr no miracle was needed for his canonization. We do have the letter he wrote to his parishioners as he awaited death:

My dear brothers and sisters, know this: Our Lord Jesus Christ upon descending into the world took innumerable pains upon and constituted the holy Church through his own passion and increases it through the passion of its faithful. . . . Now, however, some fifty or sixty years since holy Church entered into our Korea, the faithful suffer persecutions again. Even today persecution rages, so that many of our friends of the same faith, among who am I myself, have been thrown into prison. Just as you also remain in the midst of persecution. Since we have formed one body, how can we not be saddened in our innermost hearts? How can we not experience the pain of separation in our human faculties? However, as Scripture says, God cares for the least hair of our heads, and indeed he cares with his omniscience; therefore, how can persecution be considered as anything other than the command of God, or his prize, or precisely his punishment? . . . We are twenty here, and thanks be to God all are still well. If anyone is killed, I beg you not to forget his family. I have many more things to say, but how can I express them with pen and paper? I make an end to this letter. Since we are now close to the struggle, I pray you to walk in faith, so that when you have finally entered into Heaven, we may greet one another. I leave you my kiss of love.

Quote

"We have come into the world by God's grace; by that same grace we have received baptism, entrance into the Church, and the honor of being called Christians. Yet what good will this do us if we are Christians in name alone and not in fact?"

Recipe

Kimchi

Kimchi is the national dish of Korea. It is nutrient-dense from a variety of vegetables and packed with the health benefits of probiotics. It is spicy from the chili powder, sweet from fruits and sugar, sour from the fermentation process (similar to how sauerkraut is made), salty from sea salt, and contains umami from soy sauce, fish sauce, and oyster sauce.

- **PREP TIME**: About 45 minutes total
    - **BRINING / DRAINING**: 2 hours, 45 minutes
    - **FERMENTATION**: 24-48 hours
- **YIELD**: 1½-2 quarts
- **MAKE IT VEGAN** by eliminating the Fish Sauce and Oyster Sauce, replacing with Soy Sauce or your favorite similar condiment.

INGREDIENTS

1 head of Napa cabbage (about 2-3 pounds)

3 tablespoons to ½ cup Korean red chili pepper flakes (gochugaru). *Note: ½ cup of Korean chili flakes will produce a fiery, spicy kimchi. Use anywhere from 3 tablespoons for milder kimchi, and up to ½ cup for spicy kimchi)*

12-16 ounces daikon radish, cleaned and peeled

1 Asian pear (bosc pear may substitute; if none available, use a sweet apple)

2 carrots, cleaned and peeled

6 scallions / green onions

3 tablespoons grated onion – or chopped very fine

3 cloves garlic, finely chopped

1½ teaspoons peeled, grated fresh ginger root (about ½ ounce)

2 teaspoons glutinous rice flour / sweet rice flour (or choose one: potato starch / tapioca flour / corn starch)

1½ teaspoons brown sugar or white sugar

½ teaspoon soy sauce

½ teaspoon fish sauce

½ teaspoon oyster sauce (optional)

¾ cup sea salt or kosher salt for brining (non-iodized and with no caking agents added), plus optional additional salt to season kimchi.

Water: water for brining and rinsing cabbage must not be chlorinated. If in doubt, purchase 3-4 gallons spring water for brining and rinsing.

SPECIAL EQUIPMENT NEEDED

- Colander
- Large mixing bowl or large pot
- Food-safe glass or plastic container(s) with a tight-fitting lid, such as canning jars or mason jars, cleaned. This is to store your Kimchi. If using canning/mason jars, you will need either (1) Half-Gallon jar, or (2) One-Quart jars. Do not use a metal container to store Kimchi; the metal can react with the Kimchi.
- Disposable gloves (optional)

DIRECTIONS

- Before you begin, understand the importance of food safety when making Kimchi. Kimchi is not cooked, it is fermented. Therefore, harmful bacteria, dirt, and/or pathogens which would normally be destroyed during cooking can be introduced if you don't follow precautions:
- Wash your hands thoroughly with soap and water for 20 seconds whenever handling ingredients. If you have any open cuts on your hands, wear disposable gloves while working with ingredients.
- Use clean cutting boards, pots, knives and utensils. Don't cross-contaminate items. When in doubt, thoroughly clean the kitchen item or utensil, or replace with a clean one.
- Wash your produce thoroughly before peeling and/or cutting them. Cutting through unwashed produce can transfer harmful dirt or bacteria to your Kimchi.
- Your water for brining and rinsing the cabbage must not be chlorinated. Chlorine can disrupt the fermentation. If in doubt, use bottled, unchlorinated spring water.
- Always use a clean utensil when removing kimchi from the jar.
- If your kimchi ever develops spots or mold on surface – discard.

Brine the cabbage:

- Remove any discolored leaves from cabbage. Cut cabbage in half lengthwise. Rinse cabbage halves under cold water to remove any dirt, separating the leaves as you rinse. Shake off excess water. Then cut each in half again, lengthwise. Cut off the triangular, thick core at the base of each section. Then cut each piece in half again, lengthwise. (You should have 8 long sections total). Cut each section into 1-inch pieces.
- Clean your mixing bowl or pot, and fill with 6 cups cold water. Add ½ cup sea salt. Stir until salt is dissolved. Place cabbage pieces in water and stir gently so that all pieces have been submerged in brine. Leave the cabbage pieces to sit in the brine at room

temperature for 15 minutes, mixing them after about 8 minutes. Drain in colander. Do not rinse.

- Return the drained, brined cabbage to mixing bowl. Sprinkle with ¼ cup sea salt and mix into cabbage. Place a large plate on top of the cabbage, and something heavy on top of the plate to weigh it down (a large can, a brick, a paperweight). Let sit for 2 hours.

- After two hours, drain into a colander. Rinse cabbage leaves with fresh water several times, moving them around gently to rinse off all the salt. Allow to drain for 20 minutes.

Prepare the rest of ingredients (begin 40 minutes before cabbage is ready)

- Add ¾ cup water to a small pot. Stir in the rice flour (or substitute – see recipe). Simmer over low heat, stirring occasionally, until it thickens to a thin paste. Remove pot from heat to cool.

- Daikon radish: Peel the outer layer with a vegetable peeler or paring knife. Rinse. Slice into thin, ¼" rounds. Then slice into thin, matchstick-width strips.

- Carrots: Peel carrots, cut ½" off the top. Cut into 2" pieces. Then slice each piece into ⅛"- thick slices. Tip: Cut a bit off one side to create a flat surface, then proceed cutting into ⅛" slices. Stack a few slices and cut into ⅛" thin, long strips. (Or you may grate the carrots)

- Scallions: Rinse. Cut off the root ends, discard. Cut 2-3" off the green, leafy end – discard. Cut off the bulbous root (onion-shaped) and chop fine. Slice the remaining length of scallions into 1" pieces.

- Pear/Apple: Peel. Cut in half, top to bottom. Cut each piece in half again, top to bottom. Slice off the core, discard. Cut each piece into thin slices (⅛"-¼" thick). Then cut those slices into matchsticks (thin strips)

- Ginger Root: Rub off skin with a spoon. Rinse, then finely grate the ginger. If you don't have a grater, rub peeled ginger root with a spoon to "grate" it. Chop finely with a knife if needed.

Mix and Bottle your Kimchi:

- In a large mixing bowl: Add cooled rice flour paste, chopped garlic, grated onion, grated ginger, fish sauce, soy sauce, sugar, oyster sauce (optional), and your desired amount of Korean Red Chili Pepper Flakes. Stir well to combine. Add the radish, carrots, scallions and pear (or apple.)

- Put on disposable gloves. Mix by hand to combine well. If you don't have disposable gloves, use two spatulas or large spoons to mix and toss as you would a salad. Add drained, brined cabbage to bowl. Mix very well so that all cabbage pieces are evenly coated in chili mixture and all ingredients are combined. Taste a piece of cabbage, adjust ingredients for taste.
- Spoon the Kimchi into clean jar(s), pushing down to release any air bubbles and to pack the kimchi tightly. Only fill jars ⅔ full – this mixture may expand. Make sure the surface is submerged in brine. Place lids on jars very loosely: Screw on the lid until it just tightens, then loosen the lid a bit.
- Place the jar(s) in a glass or ceramic dish with sides, in case the mixture bubbles over. Leave the jar(s) out at room temperature (optimal 65-68 degrees Fahrenheit) for 24-48 hours, away from sunlight or any heat source. If your environment is hotter than that, find a cooler place in your house such as a pantry, basement, or garage.
- After 24 hours, open the jar and, using a clean utensil, taste your kimchi. If the taste is to your liking, it is ready to refrigerate. You may eat it now – it is closer to a spicy, crunchy slaw. If you like your kimchi a bit more sour/fermented, leave out at room temperature up to an additional 12-24 hours. When the taste is to your liking, pack down the kimchi in jar using a clean spoon, or your hand covered in a disposable glove, and make sure the surface kimchi is submerged in brine. Cover the lid tightly. Refrigerate.

Some notes about storing Kimchi

- Kimchi will continue to ferment as it refrigerates, just at a slower pace. It will go through flavor and texture changes. It is crunchy and spicy in the beginning, then the vegetables will begin to soften as fermentation continues. The flavor will change from bright and spicy in the beginning to a sour, earthy taste as it ages. You may notice bubbles forming in the liquid—that is the fermentation process. All are perfectly okay.
- Your kimchi can last for up to a month in your refrigerator as long as you keep it packed down and it remains submerged in liquid. Oxygenation is not good for kimchi's environment—avoid opening the jar often. Always look out for dangerous molds and bacteria: if your kimchi develops spots on it or in the jar, or if it smells "off," it is best to discard it.

Prayers

TRADITIONAL PRAYER

O God, you have created all nations and you are their salvation. In the land of Korea your call to Catholic faith formed a people of adoption, whose growth you nurtured by the blood of Andrew, Paul, and their companions. Through their martyrdom and their intercession grant us strength that we too may remain faithful to your commandments even until death. We ask this through our Lord Jesus Christ, your Son, who lives and reigns with you and the Holy Spirit, one God, for ever and ever. Amen.[3]

CONTEMPORARY PRAYER

St. Andrew Kim, from an early age you knew your mind and lived your faith. Help me to be brave enough to express my beliefs, even when they are unpopular or cause me to suffer, and help me face my trials with courage. Amen.

CHAPTER 13

St. Lydia of Thyatira

*B*rigit was standing by the wine and beer bar. "Is there any soju here?" Solanus asked.

"Not that I know of," Brigit said. "Only beer and wine. In fact, I'm going to have a beer now." She poured herself a glass and took a long draught.

"We will have to check with Martha in the kitchen about soju. If anyone can come up with a glass, it would be Martha," Solanus said to Kim. "Let's go find her."

Brigit watched as Solanus and Kim strolled to the other side of the room. "May I join you?" It was at that moment when Lydia of Thyatira walked up, the pleats of her purple stola swishing a bit around her ankles as she walked.

"Would you like beer or do you prefer wine?" Brigit asked her.

"I think I'll go with wine," Lydia replied.

"Red or white?"

"Red."

Brigit reached over and pulled a ladle from one of the large jars. She filled a glass with the ruby-red liquid. "I'm a beer girl myself."

Lydia took a sip of the wine. "An excellent vintage. But what would we expect after Cana," she laughed. "I'm going out on the patio. Teresa and some of the others are out there. They asked Solanus to let us know when the guest arrives. Wouldn't want to be like those Five Foolish Virgins, now would we?"

The two opened a side door to see Teresa, Gertrude, and Josephine Bakhita chatting under a grape arbor. The aroma of sun-warmed ripe grapes filled the air.

The name "Lydia" means "the Lydian woman," which probably indicates that she was originally from Lydia. Lydia was an area in Asia Minor in what is now modern Turkey, about forty miles across the sea from Athens. Thyatira is the ancient name of the modern city of Askisar.

• • • • • • • • • • • • • • • • •

The Parable of the Virgins is told in Matthew 25:1–13. In it, Jesus tells about five foolish and five wise virgins who were waiting for the coming of the bridegroom. The foolish virgins did not have any oil in their lamps, and when the bridegroom finally arrived, they were unable to purchase any. The take-away was to "Therefore, stay awake, for you know neither the day nor the hour."

"Come join us," Teresa said, pointing to two empty chairs. "It's lovely out here." Brigit and Lydia joined the group.

"We were just talking about the kind of challenges we faced as women," Teresa went on. "I was saying that it was sometimes difficult for me to be taken seriously about my reforms just because I was a woman. I think I had to work twice as hard as any man to get half as much accomplished." The other women nodded knowingly.

"Oh, tell me about it," Lydia said, sipping her wine. "Remember I had Paul himself to deal with!"

"That's right," Gertrude said. "He stayed at your house once, didn't he?"

"More than once. But not necessarily because he wanted to." Lydia smoothed her purple skirt.

"By the way," Teresa said, "I do like that purple color."

"Thanks," Lydia said. "I figured that if I dressed the rich and famous of my day in purple cloth, I could wear it myself up here."

Lydia is described in Acts as a "dealer in purple cloth." The color purple was reserved for royals, nobles, and high-level officials.

• •

The river in question was the Gaggitis River. Today a small chapel, used only for baptisms, is located on the traditional site.

"Sort of like my dance shoes," Teresa said, holding up her foot and showing off her boot.

"Exactly!" Lydia agreed. "Did I ever tell you about the time I won an argument with Paul?"

"Really!?" Josephine exclaimed. "I want to hear about it."

"I think I may be the only person to ever win an argument with him," Lydia said with a hint of pride. "Certainly the only woman." She took another sip of wine and settled back in her chair. "It all began when Paul and Timothy came to Philippi where I had my business. Anyway, I used to go to the river with some other women on the Sabbath to pray."

"And get away from it all," added Brigit.

"Well, that too," Lydia agreed. "We were just finishing up when this skinny kid and this bald-headed guy came up and started talking to us. At first, I was sort of put off. Who was this guy and what was he doing talking about a Messiah. But after a while, I began to get more interested in what he had to say. It was almost evening, so I suggested that we meet again the next day around noon. Now that part isn't in the 'official' account, but then I wasn't the one recording exactly what happened," she chuckled. "I'm lucky Luke put me in his book of Acts at all! Anyway, the bald guy, that was Paul, came back the next day and we talked some more. I met with him every day at noon for about a week. Finally, I decided that I wanted to be baptized. His message about the Christ really touched me. I knew that was what I had been looking for." The other women nodded in agreement. "So Paul baptized me and the members of my household." She paused. "I never forced anyone to be baptized, but some of the servants wanted to and some of my relatives. And a few of my friends. They just got all lumped into 'members of my household.'"

"Was it just women?" Gertrude asked. "Or were some men baptized too?"

"Women and men," Lydia said. "I had made my own way in the business world, so there were some men who actually respected my judgment. Even in spiritual matters. This is where it gets interesting. Paul didn't want to stay at my house. I'm not sure what his problem was. Maybe he thought it would be scandalous if he stayed at a house owned by a woman who wasn't married."

"Or maybe he was just being Paul," Teresa said.

"Maybe," Lydia agreed. "But you have to remember that he baptized me. So I said to him that if he considered me a believer, then he would come and stay at my house. You should have seen his face," she laughed. "If he refused to come, then he was saying I wasn't a believer and his baptism wasn't valid. But he accepted that my baptism was valid, then he had to come to my house. He went off in a corner and talked to Timothy for a long time. I'm not sure what they said but when they came back, Timothy told me that they had agreed to stay with me. If looks were daggers, I think I might have had a few in my back from Paul after that." She laughed, a deep and merry laugh that echoed from the centuries. "I just love how Luke puts it: 'She prevailed on us.' More like beat Paul at his own game."

"He must have forgiven you," Josephine said. "He came and stayed with you at another time, didn't he?"

"Yes," Lydia said. "After he and Silas were released from prison they stayed at my house for a while. My home became the first church in the area." She took another sip of wine. "I wish you could have heard Paul's sermons. He was truly one of a kind."

"Well, ladies," Gertrude said. "I hate to leave you, but I need see a man about a cat," she added, as she headed back to the main room.

Did You Know?

Lydia was Paul's first convert at Philippi, the city to which he later sent his famous letter to the Philippians.

St. Lydia of Thyatira

FIRST CENTURY

Nothing is known about Lydia outside what we are told in Acts 16. We know she lived at Philippi, which was a cosmopolitan Roman colony. We also learn she was a *porfiropolis*, or "a dealer in purple cloth," "a worshiper of God," and "the Lord opened her heart to pay attention to what Paul was saying." She and "her household," which probably contained both adults and children, were baptized, and she convinced Paul to stay with her.

From those meager facts, we can deduce that she was a very wealthy woman, since purple dye was literally worth more than its weight in gold at the time. A person who dealt either in the dye or in cloth colored with the dye would have been in the top one percent economically.

Since no man is mentioned, it is assumed that Lydia was the sole owner of the business. Although some have suggested she might have been a widow, there is nothing to indicate that in the text. By calling her "god-fearing," Paul seems to indicate that she was attracted to Judaism but had not converted to that faith. Finally, we can feel relatively confident that she spoke at least two languages—Greek with Paul and the Latin that was used in Philippi.

She is called "Equal to the Apostles" in the Orthodox Church and is commemorated on August 3.

Tyrian purple, also called royal or imperial purple, is a dye obtained from the mucus of one of three varieties of sea snails. Depending on the snail, the color varies from purple-red to purple-blue to indigo. The dye can be collected by "milking" the snails, aka poking them until they secrete mucus, or by crushing them. In any event, obtaining the dye was prohibitively expensive. According to the historian B. Caseau, it took 10,000 to 12,000 snails to obtain one gram of dye, which is enough to color only the hem of a single garment. While it is difficult to translate ancient monetary values, based on a price edict from the time of the Emperor Diocletian, one pound of purple dye would be about $25,000 in modern times and a pound of dyed wool about $7,000.

Legends, Lore, and Miracles

Since the only mention we have of Lydia is in the Bible and no legends, lore, or miracles have been associated with her, we will digress here to share a few stories associated with her friend St. Paul.

Paul is described in the Acts of Paul, an early non-canonical work, as being slight in stature, bow-legged and bald, with a big nose and a unibrow. All the early portraits of him show him as bald, but not all have a unibrow. The earliest known image of him dates to the fourth century.

It is said that the head of St. Paul was thrown in a common pit after he was beheaded. A shepherd saw a light coming from the pit and excavated an illuminated head. When this head was placed at the feet of St. Paul, his body turned around and thus the head was restored to its proper place. In 2009, bones found under the Basilica of St. Paul Outside the Walls in Rome were declared by the Vatican to be those of Paul. Along with the bones, archaeologists found some incense and a piece of "purple cloth."

In 2 Corinthians 12:7–9, Paul speaks of a "thorn in the flesh." While this is often taken to mean a slight annoyance, the word used for *thorn* can also mean "tent peg," so whatever it was that Paul asked be removed might have been more burdensome than we think.

The Acts of the Apostles records several miracles performed by Paul. These include healing a crippled man, a woman possessed by an evil spirit, raising a man from the dead, and healing the sick on the island of Malta. One of his lesser known miracles is described in Acts 28:3–6, when a viper that had been hiding in a bundle of firework "fastened itself" on Paul's hand. He shook the snake into the fire and went about his business even though the people expected him to fall dead. (Note: it is possible this is less a miracle and more a matter of biology since vipers are now known to "dry bite," meaning they bite without releasing any venom, about twenty-five percent of the time.)

Quote

"If you have judged me to be faithful to the Lord,
come into my house, and stay."

Pomegranate and Pistachio Turkish Delight

Pomegranates and pistachios have been favorites in the Middle East for millennia. In fact, pistachios are among the foods Jacob told his sons to take with them to Egypt in Genesis 43:11. These delicious candies are like ruby jewels, studded with pieces of toasted pistachios.

- **PREP TIME:** 10 minutes
- **COOK TIME:** 75-90 minutes, plus overnight to set
- **YIELD:** About 30 bite-sized cubes
- **VERY HELPFUL:** Candy thermometer. Pastry bush for washing down sugar crystals (helpful, but covering the pot with a lid will suffice). Heat-proof spatula for stirring. You will need two pots: One medium-large pot with high sides and one medium-small heavy pot with high sides and a lid.
- **THIS RECIPE IS VEGAN AND GLUTEN-FREE.**

INGREDIENTS

⅓ cup shelled pistachios, chopped.
Neutral oil for coating pan and knife,
    such as sunflower, canola, or safflower.

Candy syrup:
3½ cups sugar
¼ cup light corn syrup
1¼ cups water
2 teaspoons lemon juice

Sugar coating:
½ cup powdered sugar
3 tablespoons cornstarch

Cornstarch thickener:
2¼ cups pomegranate juice
1½ cups cornstarch
1 teaspoon cream of tartar

DIRECTIONS

- Oil the inside of an 8" x 8" or 9" x 9" square baking pan liberally with a neutral oil. Line the pan with aluminum foil, leaving overhang of about 4" on all sides to act as handles. Smooth out and liberally oil the aluminum foil.

Pan-toast the chopped pistachios:

- Place chopped pistachios in a dry sauté pan over medium-high heat. Stir constantly until they begin to toast; this only takes a few minutes. Remove from heat to cool.

Make the candy syrup:

- Mix the sugar, corn syrup, water, and lemon juice in a medium-sized, heavy saucepan over medium-high heat. Stir until the sugar is dissolved. Use a wet pastry brush to wash down any sugar crystals on the sides of pan. OR place a lid on the pan until steam forms and washes any sugar crystals away and remove lid. Attach a candy thermometer to the pan. Reduce heat to low, and simmer without stirring, until the mixture reaches the soft-ball stage (240°-245° Fahrenheit). Immediately remove pan from heat.

If you don't have a candy thermometer:

- Have a glass of ice water ready. Remove ice. Drizzle a bit of candy syrup into the cold water. If you can form a ball of syrup in the cold water, and the ball flattens when removed from the water, it is ready.

Make the cornstarch thickener:

- While the syrup above is cooking: Whisk pomegranate juice with cornstarch and cream of tartar in a high-sided medium-large pot. Place pot over medium-low heat and stir constantly with a heat-proof spatula or spoon until it forms a thick paste. Keep stirring constantly—it can thicken on the bottom quickly and you want to keep this mixture smooth and incorporated. Remove from heat when it is thickened, about 7-10 minutes. Note: If your mixture begins to thicken too quickly, reduce heat. If your mixture is lumpy when done, strain through a fine-meshed sieve placed over a container, forcing as much as possible through the sieve by pressing and dragging at the same time through the sieve. Scrape off bottom of sieve into container as well. Then put this back in your pot. (If pot also has lumps in it, wash and dry before placing the thickened cornstarch/pomegranate juice mixture back in the pot.)

Add the candy syrup:
- Gradually pour the candy syrup into the cooked cornstarch mixture a bit at a time, whisking constantly until incorporated. Once all the syrup is added to your cornstarch mixture, place over low heat and cook for 45-60 minutes, stirring fairly constantly with a heat-proof spatula or spoon. The mixture will have thickened considerably when done, taking on the consistency of stiff caramel. It will go through stages of bubbling, then large, thick bubbles, then it begins to take form, coming away from the sides of the pan and forming a mass. At that point, remove from heat and stir in toasted chopped pistachios.

Turn into the pan and cool:
- Immediately pour mixture into prepared baking pan, scraping all mixture from the pot. Tap the pan onto counter-top to even out the mixture. Allow to cool and set overnight at room temperature, uncovered.

Cut and coat the cubes:
- The next day, line a baking sheet with parchment paper. Mix the remaining sugar and cornstarch (sugar coating) in a bowl, and sprinkle about one quarter of it onto the parchment-lined pan. Pick up the Turkish Delight by the tin foil "handles" and turn out onto the pan. Pull the aluminum foil off slowly. Sprinkle the top of Turkish Delight with some of the sugar/cornstarch mixture. Use a sharp, oiled knife to cut into bite-sized cubes.

Note: If your Turkish Delight is more of a caramel consistency, turn out onto an oiled plate or pan. Pull off a bite-sized amount and roll into balls using clean, oiled hands. Place a few balls at a time into the bowl of sugar/cornstarch mixture, lightly tossing to coat evenly. Store in airtight container for up to 10 days.

Prayers

TRADITIONAL PRAYER

Pour out upon us, Lord, the spirit of knowledge and love of you, with which you filled your handmaid blessed Lydia, so that, serving you sincerely in imitation of her, we may be pleasing to you by our faith and our works. Through our Lord Jesus Christ, your Son, who lives and reigns with you in the unity of the Holy Spirit, one God, forever and ever. Amen. [4]

CONTEMPORARY PRAYER

St. Lydia, may I follow your example to be unafraid to speak my mind, do what I believe is right, and live a holy life, not removed from the world, but in the midst of it. Amen.

CHAPTER 14

St. Gertrude of Nivelles

ertrude searched the dining room, looking for Martin de Porres. Finally, she caught a glimpse of him as Martha opened the kitchen door to bring out what looked like a stew. She found him leaning up against the back wall. "Martin," she said, "I need to talk to you."

Martin looked up and patted his sleeve a bit nervously. "Of course, how can I be of assistance?"

"I'm told that you know something about animals," Gertrude said firmly.

"A little," he said modestly.

"Well, I need to know everything you can tell me about cats," she said.

Martin looked a bit puzzled. "I'm happy to help, but exactly why are you asking about cats?"

Gertrude harrumphed and then sighed. "I guess I'm now the patron of them." Martin raised an eyebrow, but he let her continue. "I'm not entirely sure how it happened," she went on. "I mean, my nuns and I had cats to keep the mice and rats away from the monastery. Mice and rats are very unsanitary, you know." Martin pulled his arm closer to his side as he nodded. "Can we get out of here?" she asked suddenly. "It's very hot in here with the oven and all." Without waiting for an answer, she pushed open the kitchen door, nearly knocking Martha over in the process. "There, that's better," she said, standing in front of the place set for the guest of honor. "I wonder when our honored guest will arrive?" she asked, and then, without waiting for an answer, continued. "Now about cats."

"Before we get into that," Martin said, "please explain to me why you are now the patron of cats . . . and cat lovers, I assume."

Gertrude looked a little exasperated as she began. "If I were going to be the patron of something to do with animals, I'd have thought it would be against rats and mice." Martin interlocked his arms against his chest as she went on. "I've never liked rodents. I can't imagine anyone liking them."

All of a sudden, Gertrude looked about. "Did you hear that?"

"Hear what?"

During the Black Plague, people asked Gertrude to intercede against the rodents they believed carried the Plague. It was actually carried by fleas that lived on the rats and mice. Plague is believed to have been present somewhere in Europe every year between 1346 and 1671. In the modern era, while antibiotics and a vaccine have greatly reduced the risk, thousands were infected in another outbreak in Madagascar as recently as 2017.

• • • • • • • • • • • • • • • • • • • •

Medieval artists often portrayed souls in Purgatory as mice. When drawing pictures of Gertrude, they frequently showed her with mice or rats at her feet, indicating her care for the dead and her prayers for their salvation. She was still linked to mice as late as 1822, when little silver or gold statues of mice were being left at her shrine in Cologne.

• • • • • • • • • • • • • • • • • • • •

Metropolitan Cats by John P. O'Neill (1982) featured artwork from the Met, along with commentary. It was apparently in this review/exhibit that Gertrude was first called the patron saint of cats. Some people speculate that Gertrude might have been conflated with the Germanic goddess Frigg, who was sometimes shown riding a cat and thus became associated with cats in folklore.

"I heard a squeak. It sounded like a mouse." Gertrude stared intently at Martin's sleeve.

"I don't hear anything," Martin said.

"Hmmm," Gertrude made a slightly displeased sound and glanced nervously at the floor.

"Perhaps I was just imagining it. Anyway, I'm really not sure how I got associated with cats. The first I heard of it was just recently when I started getting all these prayer requests for help with sick kittens. The day I got thirty-five prayer requests, I knew something was up. I checked with Peter because he was processing requests that day, and he didn't have a clue. We thought it might have been a mistake, but the prayers kept coming. Eventually, I figured out that it had something to do with a museum in New York, of all places."

"Do you mind being the patron of cats?" Martin asked.

Gertrude pursed her lips. "Not really, but it's just that I don't know all that much about them."

"Cats are hard to describe," Martin said. "It's said that dogs see us as their masters, but cats see us as their slaves. Not that they can't be wonderful loving companions. It's just they are very independent. They know what they want, and they don't put up with much nonsense. Much like you," he added.

Gertrude smiled wryly. "I couldn't afford to. When you are the one in charge of a monastery, you have to be on top of things."

"You were actually in charge of a double monastery, weren't you?" Martin asked.

"Yes," she said. "But it really began with my mother. She was the one who taught me how to be strong." She smiled at the memory. "My mother was an amazing woman. I learned everything I know about being an abbess from her. I invited her to this party, but she said that she would prefer to study the pictures in clouds. She tells me that they look quite different from the top down, so to speak. She did help me prepare my potluck dish, though. She always was a better cook than I was."

Frankish double monasteries in which both men and women lived, although in separate areas, were almost always led by an abbess or jointly by an abbess and abbot. It is thought that Gertrude governed Nivelles alone because it was said she took the "whole burden of governing upon herself alone."

"Did you like being abbess?" Martin asked, in an attempt to steer the conversation as far away from mice and cats as possible.

"Yes, and no," Gertrude answered truthfully. "I would rather have spent my time in reading and study instead of administration. Did you know that I memorized much of Scripture as well as books on canon law?"

"No," Martin said. "That's quite impressive."

"But I did enjoy building churches and I loved collecting relics of the saints. Isn't it funny that I, who used to collect relics of the saints, would become a saint myself?" She laughed at the thought. "But enough reminiscing. What I really need to know about are cats."

"I would suggest you visit the Rainbow Bridge and ask . . ." Martin began, but he was interrupted by John the Baptist.

"Salted locusts?" John offered, holding out a dish to Gertrude and Martin. Both shook their heads.

Did You Know?

St. Gertrude shares a feast day with St. Patrick of Ireland.

➤ BIOGRAPHY
St. Gertrude of Nivelles
628 – MARCH 17, 659

G ertrude's father, Pepin of Landen, was a nobleman of the Frankish Empire, the largest post-Roman kingdom in Western Europe up through the early Middle Ages. It was located in what is now France, Belgium, and Germany. Because of his connections with the king, Pepin moved his family to the king's court. It was there that Gertrude first showed the spunk and determination that would characterize her life.

The name Gertrude means either "spear" or "strength."

At this time, marriages were important to consolidate power and were more political alliances than love affairs. For instance, Gertrude's sister, Begga, was married to the youngest son of a royal counselor, an arrangement that paved the way for a later shift of power through the marriages of her sons. When Gertrude was ten, the king asked if she would like to marry the son of a duke. Gertrude not only declined, but she did so with force, with an early biography reporting she "lost her temper and flatly rejected him with an oath," saying she would be married only to Christ. Whether she actually made a pledge for virginity at that age or not, Gertrude never married, although many attempted to marry her for the sake of her wealth and standing.

A monastery is the residence and working quarters of either monks or nuns. In modern usage, the word *monastery* is generally applied only to a community of monks, and the word *convent* is used for a community of nuns. The word "nunnery" is a slang term for a community of nuns and was used for either a convent or a monastery. In Shakespeare's time, it was another name for a brothel, hence the play on words when Hamlet tells Ophelia to "get thee to a nunnery."

When her father died, Gertrude's mother, Itta, made a bold choice to ensure the safety of herself and her daughter from those who wanted to force Gertrude into marriage (and herself into remarriage). She is said to have shaved Gertrude's hair into a tonsure, indicating that she was dedicated to God, and then she built a monastery for them to live in.

The earliest account of Gertrude's life, called her *Vita*, says that Itta had worried about what would happen to them when Bishop Armand, commonly called St. Armand, came to Itta as "preaching the word of God. At the Lord's bidding, he asked whether she would build a monastery for herself and Christ's handmaid, Gertrude." Itta promptly ordered the construction of a monastery for both men and women at Nivelles, where she and Gertrude could live in relative peace. Itta governed the monastery for about twelve years, until she died at age sixty, after which Gertrude took over.

During her tenure as Abbess, Gertrude frequently welcomed guests, especially Irish monks who traveled to mainland Europe as missionaries. Among the most notable of these were St. Foillan and his brother Ultan, who stayed at Nivelles on their way to Peronne in Northern France to visit the grave of their brother Fursey. Foillan, Ultan, and Fursey were early medieval Irish missionary/monks who did much to spread Christianity, especially in East Anglia. Gertrude gave land to St. Foillan and St. Ultan to build a monastery at Fosses, Belgium.

> The Abbey at Nivelles was bombed during the Battle of Belgium in May 1940 but was restored after World War II.

Like many saints, Gertrude compromised her health through her penances, which included abstaining from food and sleep and wearing a hair shirt. These severe penances may be attributed to the influence of Irish monasticism. When her health grew too bad, she was forced to resign as Abbess in December 658 at the age of thirty-two.

She appointed her niece, Wulfetrude, as her successor. Gertrude died on March 17, 659, and was almost immediately declared a saint. Her feast day (March 17) was declared by Pope Clement in 1677. She is the patron of travelers, gardeners, mental illness, and, unofficially—cats.

Legends, Lore, and Miracles

St. Gertrude of Nivelles is often confused with St. Gertrude the Great. Gertrude the Great was a German Benedictine nun who lived in the thirteenth century. Traditional images of Gertrude of Nivelles show her with mice running up her staff of office as abbess, but virtually all contemporary images now show her holding a cat.

Water from the well at the monastery at Nivelles was said to chase away rodents when sprinkled in an area.

It is said that the day before she died, Gertrude asked St. Ultan if he knew when she was going to die. He said that she would die the next day during Mass, and St. Patrick himself would be watching over her deathbed.

Many stories surround the three monk brothers Foillan, Ultan, and Fursey, and Gertrude. In one, after saying Mass in Nivelles, Foillan went on a journey to an unknown destination. Along the way, he and his companions were robbed and murdered. When news of his disappearance reached his monastery, the monks began to search for him. They were unsuccessful, but Gertrude found his body seventy-seven days after his murder, on the exact anniversary of their brother Fursey's death. She had the body returned to Fosses for burial.

In another legend, Gertrude guaranteed safe ocean passage for a group of travelers who were "peacefully sailing over the sea on the monastery's business." When a storm and a sea monster tried to capsize their boat, they called on Gertrude for protection. Instantly the sea calmed and the monster disappeared. Because of this myth, medieval travelers drank a toast to Gertrude before starting their journey. Even now in Belgium, a final drink for the night is called a "St. Gertrude's Cup."

One miracle attributed to Gertrude occurred when she was standing before the altar in the Church. Her *Vita* says, "She saw descending above her a flaming pellucid sphere such that the whole basilica was illuminated by its brightness." The author of the *Vita* speculates that this vision was a "visitation of the True Light."

Quote

"I have chosen for my spouse him, from whose eternal beauty all creatures derive their glory, whose riches are immense, and whom the angels adore."

Recipe

———⟫◈⟪———

Eggs Baked with Bacon, Cabbage, and Leeks

Meals in Gertrude's monastery were simple but wholesome. Eggs, cabbage, and leeks were often eaten with meat such as bacon added on special occasions. The egg mixture bakes in a hot water bath, a method that was referenced as early as the first century after Christ in the ancient Roman cookbook Apicius.

- **PREP TIME:** 20 minutes
- **COOK TIME:** Bake time: 1 hour, plus 35 minutes total to cook bacon and cabbage/leeks.
- **SERVES:** 6-8 people
- **SPECIAL EQUIPMENT:** Ovenproof casserole dish, 3-quart size preferred. Or you can use individual ramekins or two smaller casserole dishes. Large roasting pan, or pan larger than your baking dish to serve as a water bath.
- **MAKE IT LACTO-OVO VEGETARIAN** by excluding the bacon and using butter or your favorite cooking oil instead of bacon fat.

INGREDIENTS

½ pound sliced bacon (about 9 slices)

1 leek

1 small head cabbage or 2 cups packed shredded raw cabbage

¼ teaspoon celery seed (optional)

1 dozen eggs, medium

½ cup milk or heavy cream

½ teaspoon sea salt, divided

¼ teaspoon black pepper, divided

½ cup shredded cheese such as Swiss, Cheddar, Havarti, or Gruyere

DIRECTIONS

Cook the bacon: Preheat oven to 400 degrees Fahrenheit.

- Line a cookie sheet with parchment paper or tinfoil. Line pieces of bacon on cookie sheet. Do not overlap bacon. Bake for 18-20 minutes, or until bacon is crisp.
- Remove from oven. Set bacon on paper towels to drain. Drain the bacon fat into a heatproof bowl or cup and reserve.

Prepare the leek:

- Cut the root end off the leek, discard root.
  Cut the dark green leafy end off the leek, discard.
- Slice the leek in half, lengthwise. Then slice into thin pieces.
- Place the sliced leeks in a bowl and fill with cold water. Move the leeks around to remove any sand, which will settle to the bottom.
- Remove leeks from bowl, shaking off excess water, and place on a few layers of paper towel to drain.

Prepare the cabbage:

- Remove outer leaves of cabbage. Slice off the root.
  Cut cabbage in half, root to top.
- Rinse cabbage under cold water to clean. Shake and let drain
- Cut each piece in half again, root to top. Slice off the hard, thick root portion.
- Slice the cabbage ¼" thick, then rough chop the slices.

Cook the cabbage and leeks

- Heat a very large frying pan over medium-high heat. Add a tablespoon of reserved bacon fat to the pan. Add leeks and cabbage. Season with celery seed (optional), ⅛ teaspoon black pepper and ¼ teaspoon sea salt. Cook for 10-15 minutes, stirring occasionally, until the cabbage and leeks are tender.
- Season to taste.

Make the Dish.

- Preheat oven to 350 degrees, with rack in center of oven.
- Grease a 3-quart casserole (or equivalent size baking dish) lightly with bacon grease. You may also use individual ramekins or two smaller casserole dishes.
- Have a roasting / baking pan large enough to hold the casserole dish with room to spare on the side. The pan should have sides so it can accommodate a water bath.
- Beat in a large bowl: the eggs, milk or heavy cream, ¼ teaspoon salt and ⅛ teaspoon black pepper together until well blended.
- Place the empty casserole dish in the roasting pan. Place the cabbage/leek mixture on bottom of casserole dish. Sprinkle with shredded cheese. Crumble the bacon over the cheese. Pour the egg mixture over everything.
- Place the roasting pan containing the casserole dish in oven.

- Carefully add very hot tap water to the roasting pan until the water is halfway up the sides of the casserole dish. Avoid getting water in the egg dish.
- Bake for one hour.
- Remove pan carefully from oven, then remove casserole from water bath. Serve.

Prayers

We do not have any prayers written by or associated with Gertrude of Nivelles, but this, from the Breastplate of St. Patrick, is a close representation of her faith.

I arise today
Through God's strength to pilot me;
God's might to uphold me,
God's wisdom to guide me,
God's eye to look before me,
God's ear to hear me,
God's word to speak for me,
God's hand to guard me,
God's way to lie before me,
God's shield to protect me,
God's hosts to save me
Afar and anear,
Alone or in a multitude.

CONTEMPORARY PRAYER

St. Gertrude, help to me to welcome guests with joy and serve with humility. And, please, while you are listening, could you spare a little care for dear cat (name) as well? Amen.

CHAPTER 15

St. Martha of Bethany

Martha wiped her hands on her apron. She had used a little quantum physics to change a glass of wine to soju for Kim. *Not quite as good as transforming whole jars of water to wine*, she thought, *but not bad for a first attempt at making something I've never heard of.* Kim seemed pleased when he tasted it.

She opened the door and surveyed the buffet table. She didn't like potlucks; you couldn't control what people brought, and all too often you ended up with all desserts and no main dishes. This time it was the salads that were missing. In keeping with her take-charge character, she thought, *It would have been a lot easier if I had just been allowed to assign dishes to people, but I can find something in the garden.* Her sister, Mary, had liked salads when she was on earth, but her brother, Lazarus, had loved the lamb stew she had brought as her potluck offering.

She slipped out the back door of the kitchen past the patio to the potager garden and began looking for vegetables to make a quick green salad. She could hear voices coming from the patio on the other side of the cottage, but she quickly ignored them. *No time to waste on chitchat*, she thought. *The guest will be here before we know it.*

She hummed to herself as she picked lettuce, radishes, and onions. At the last minute, she picked a few borage flowers as well. The garden was warm in the sunshine, and she thought about just staying out there, but then her sense of duty took over, and she gathered up her skirts and returned to the kitchen. She was washing the vegetables when Martin stuck his head through the doorway.

The name *Martha* comes from the Aramaic word meaning "the mistress" or "the lady." She apparently was in charge of her own household, since Luke 10:38 says that "Jesus entered a village where a woman whose name was Martha welcomed him."

• •

Potager is the French word for a kitchen garden. A potager contains vegetables, culinary and medicinal herbs, as well as the occasional fruits. It is designed to be as pleasing to look at as it is to be functional, so the plants are often arranged in an artistic manner, and flowers are frequently included as decorative elements.

A wide variety of vegetables were grown or gathered in first-century Israel. Leeks, garlic, onions, radishes, and lettuce were common. Melons, including muskmelons and watermelons, were also grown, although the watermelons were generally much less sweet than the current varieties. Mushrooms were harvested in season, as were field greens such as saltbush.

• • • • • • • • • • • • • • • • • •

Borage, sometimes called starflower, is an edible annual herb with star-shaped pink-blue flowers. The leaves have a cucumber-like flavor, while the flowers have a sweeter, more honey-like taste.

"Need any help?" he asked.

Martha started to refuse, then changed her mind. "Actually, yes. I could use a hand." She handed him a bunch of dripping lettuce. "Please dry these off and tear them into pieces." As he took the leafy greens, she explained, "There don't seem to be enough fresh vegetables on the buffet. It's important to have fresh vegetables, you know." Martin nodded as he wrapped the greens in a towel and shook them gently. "I'm not sure how much time we have, so I thought I'd just make a quick salad." Picking up a knife, she began to chop the other vegetables and toss them into a large bowl. As soon as Martin had finished drying the greens, she added them to the bowl and tossed them gently. "Now for a dressing," she said mostly to herself.

"Oil and vinegar are always good," Martin suggested, handing her a bottle of olive oil.

"Good idea," Martha agreed and began to mix the oil with some vinegar and spices. She poured the mixture over the salad and garnished it with the borage flowers—just to make it look pretty. "There," she said with satisfaction.

"I'll put it on the table for you," Martin said, taking the bowl and returning to the dining room.

Alone again in the kitchen, Martha pulled up a low stool and sat down with a plop. Her feet hurt, she decided, and her shoulders, too. *I didn't think feet and shoulders were supposed to hurt in heaven,* she thought. The kitchen door opened, and Martha expected to see Martin, but instead, she was surprised by Gertrude.

"I'm sorry to bother you," Gertrude said, "but I'm looking for Martin. I thought he might still be here in the kitchen. I have a couple of things I want to discuss."

Martha shook her head. "He was, but he took a salad out to the buffet table."

Gertrude said, "I must have missed him again," as she pulled up a stool and sat down next to Martha. "By any chance, do you know anything about cats?"

"I do," Martha said. "We had cats protecting the grain when I was on earth. I was particularly fond of one I called Miu-miu." Her eyes took on a dreamy expression. "He was tiger-striped and an excellent mouser. Why do you ask?"

"It's a long story how I got involved with cats," Gertrude said. "But you said you had cats. I don't remember cats being mentioned in the Bible."

"They aren't," Martha agreed. "But that doesn't mean we didn't keep cats around. Or rather that cats didn't keep us around," she laughed. "I'm not sure that anyone ever really tames a cat. They just agree to let us take care of them. But you really should talk to Martin about them. He used to take cats to his sister's house."

"That's exactly why I need to find him," Gertrude said. "We had been talking about cats earlier, and he mentioned something about a 'Rainbow Bridge.' I need to ask him a few more questions about it."

"Rainbow Bridge?" Martha questioned as she stood up and stretched her back. "I've been here forever and there are still areas I haven't explored. That's one of them. Do let me know what you find out about it."

The ancient Egyptian word for a male cat is *miu* or *mii*. The feminine form is *milt*. When pronounced, both versions sound like the English word for a cat's cry—meow.

• •

Wild cats are known to have lived among the people of ancient Mesopotamia since at least 12,000 BC, roughly the same time that dogs, sheep, and goats were domesticated. Cat remains dating back around 7000 BC have been found in Neolithic Jericho and other prehistoric sites in ancient Israel. The skeleton of a cat was found in a grave dating to 9500 BC on the island of Cyprus. Since the island had no native cats, it is assumed the animal was brought there as a companion. One reason that cats may not be mentioned in the Bible is that they were worshiped as gods in ancient Egypt, and the authors of the Bible might have wanted to avoid the references.

Luke 10:36–42 tells of a time when Jesus was staying at Martha's house. Her sister, Mary, left all the work, presumably the preparation for a meal, to Martha while she listened to Jesus speak. When Martha complained and asked Jesus to tell Mary to come help, he said, "Martha, Martha, you are anxious and worried about many things. There is need of only one thing. Mary has chosen the better part and it will not be taken from her."

• • • • • • • • • • • • • • • • • • • •

A tichel is a kind of headscarf worn by Jewish women. While it is not known exactly what sort of veil or scarf women wore in Martha's time, it is known that respectable women generally covered their hair when in public.

"You might ask Martin yourself if we ever see him again," Gertrude said. "I swear that man can disappear faster than the blink of an eye."

"Teleportation," Martha said sagely. "He thinks we don't notice, but he uses it all the time," she chuckled.

"Well," Gertrude said, standing up and dusting off her habit. "I guess I'll go see if I can find him. You will be joining us for dinner, won't you?"

Martha made a little murmuring sound that could have been either agreement or disagreement, as Gertrude left the kitchen. *I think I'll just stay right here,* she thought. *I've always been more comfortable in the kitchen.* She began humming to herself again as she drew a sink full of soapy water and began to do the dishes.

"What are you doing?" Teresa of Avila's voice startled Martha and she almost dropped the plate she was washing. "You can't stay in here."

Martha turned and put her hands on her hips. "Why not?"

"You know why not," Teresa said. "You weren't supposed to be in the kitchen anyway. That's the whole point of a potluck. No one has to do all the cooking. Do you really want to get scolded again?" she asked pointedly.

"Come on. Let me help you pin up your hair so that you look decent." Teresa pulled an ornate hairpin from her own curls and tucked Martha's graying hair into a low bun at the nape of her neck. "Now, where's your tichel?" Martha pointed to a yellow and brown veil hanging on the edge of a cupboard.

Teresa arranged the scarf so that its embroidered hem was clearly visible. "How did you learn to do that?" Martha asked.

"Remember my grandfather was Jewish," Teresa said. "Besides, I've always loved fashion." She stood back and looked at Martha. "You look wonderful. Now let's go out and get ready to meet the guest of honor." She held open the kitchen door. "After you, my friend!"

Did You Know?

There are at least three Marys mentioned in the Gospels. Sometimes Mary of Bethany is confused with Mary Magdalene.

➤ BIOGRAPHY

St. Martha of Bethany

FIRST CENTURY

W hile we have three accounts of Martha of Bethany's interactions with Jesus in the Gospels, we actually don't know much about her. Her story is always told in conjunction with that of her sister, Mary, and their brother, Lazarus. The first mention of Martha (and Mary) occurs when Martha complains that Mary is spending too much time listening to Jesus and not enough time helping in the kitchen. The second is after the death of Lazarus, and finally, we are told that "Martha served" at a dinner where Jesus's feet were anointed with expensive perfume.

Bethany, known today as Al-Eizariya or al-Azariya, is a town in today's West Bank, less than two miles from Jerusalem. Its Arabic name means "place of Lazarus," a reference to the biblical Lazarus. It has been inhabited since the sixth century BC and is mentioned eleven times in the Bible.

• •

During biblical times, people did not sit at tables with chairs like we do today. Instead, they reclined on coaches situated around a low table. For those who followed the Roman fashion, three couches were set around a central table. The host would recline on the middle couch, and guests would recline on the couches on either side. Participants would lie on their left elbows, using their right hands to eat. Their feet would be stretched out behind them, making it convenient for Jesus to wash the feet of his disciples at the Last Supper if they used this arrangement. Incidentally, the place of honor was at the left of the host, which is where Judas was seated.

We also learn that she is not afraid to speak her mind to Jesus, asking him to tell her sister to help her and then, at Lazarus's death, confronting him by saying, "Lord, if you had been here, my brother would not have died." And then, when he is about to command Lazarus to come out of the tomb, she plainly states, "Lord, by now there will be a stench; he has been dead for four days." Her outspoken nature is equally apparent when she boldly proclaims, "I have come to believe that you are the Messiah, the Son of God, the one who is coming into the world."

The third mention of Martha occurs "six days before Passover." Jesus is in attendance at a dinner given in his honor in which Lazarus is "reclining at table with him" and "Martha served."

Their sister, Mary, took about a pint of nard and used it to perfume Jesus's feet, prompting Judas to complain that the perfume should have been sold and the money given to the poor since it was worth a year's wages.

After this incident, Martha disappears from the biblical record, although numerous legends attempt to explain what happened next. She is remembered on July 29 and is the patron of numerous activities, most of which involve the domestic arts, including cooks, dietitians, servants, homemakers, hotel keepers, housemaids, laundry workers, and butlers.

Nard, also called spikenard, was an herbal oil used as a perfume in biblical times. The coat of arms of Pope Francis contains a sprig of spikenard, a reference to St. Joseph in Hispanic iconography.

Legends, Lore, and Miracles

One of the most prevalent legends about Martha says that she and her sister, Mary, and her brother, Lazarus, left Judea after Jesus's resurrection and went to the area of Avignon, France. A thirteenth-century collection of hagiographies compiled by Jacobus de Voragine, *The Golden Legend*, recounts their story:

Saint Martha, hostess of our Lord Jesus Christ, was born of a royal kindred. Her father was named Syro and her mother Encharia. The father of her was duke of Syria and places maritime, and Martha with her sister possessed by the heritage of their mother three places, that was, the castle Magdalen, and Bethany and a part of Jerusalem. It is nowhere read that Martha had ever any husband nor fellowship of man, but she as a noble hostess ministered and served our Lord, and would also that her sister should serve him and help her, for she thought that all the world was not sufficient to serve such a guest.

After the ascension of our Lord, when the disciples were departed, she with her brother Lazarus and her sister Mary, also Saint Maximin [actually a third-century figure] which baptized them, and to whom they were committed of the Holy Ghost, and many others, were put into a ship without sail, oars, or rudder, by the pagans, which by the conduct of our Lord they came all to Marseilles, and after came to the territory of Aquense or Aix, and there converted the people to the faith. Martha was right eloquent of speech, and courteous and gracious to the sight of the people.

Another legend says that Martha spent some time in Tarascon, France. There a monstrous dragon with a lion's head and a snake's tail lived in a forest between Arles and Avignon. It is claimed it terrorized the population with its sword-sharp teeth and horns until Martha held up a cross, sprinkled the beast with holy water, and led it peacefully into the village.

In the Orthodox tradition, Martha is one of the women who brought spices to anoint the body of Jesus in the tomb and thus was one of the first to witness the Resurrection. In this tradition, Martha, Mary, and Lazarus traveled to Cyprus, where he became a bishop.

Quote
"(But) even now I know that whatever you ask of God, God will give you."

Recipe

———⟫·◆·⟪———

Oven-Baked Lamb and Rosemary Stew

This lamb and stew is an ode to Martha, patron saint of cooks and servants, and a nod to her sister, Mary, with use of rosemary. Lamb was eaten on special occasions and at Passover. Jesus is called the "lamb of God."

- **PREP TIME:** 25 minutes
- **COOK TIME:** 25 minutes on stovetop plus 2 to 2½ hours in oven
- **SERVES:** 8 people
- **SPECIAL EQUIPMENT:** A Dutch Oven is preferred, but a heavy roasting pan covered with foil and a small vent hole cut into middle of foil would substitute. Or cook as you would a stew, using a covered pot on stovetop (low heat); or in a slow cooker (8 hours slow cooker time)
- **NOTE:** Use oven mitts or potholders when grasping handles on a Dutch Oven, even when cooking on a stovetop.
- **MAKE IT GLUTEN-FREE** by using gluten-free beef stock and gluten-free flour. Ensure that your red wine vinegar (typically naturally gluten-free) and lamb are also processed without gluten.

INGREDIENTS

1 tablespoon fresh rosemary,
   stems removed, finely chopped
   or ¾ teaspoon dried rosemary,
   crushed
2 pounds lamb shoulder,
   trimmed of fat, cut into 2" cubes
¾ teaspoon salt
¼ teaspoon pepper
Flour to coat lamb cubes,
   approximately ½ cup

4-5 tablespoons olive oil
2 cups red wine
1 medium yellow onion, chopped
2 garlic cloves, finely chopped
2 cups low-sodium beef stock (and
   up to ¾ cup additional)
2 tablespoons red wine vinegar
2 cups baby carrots

DIRECTIONS

Place rack in center of oven and preheat oven to 350 degrees.

- Pick the rosemary off the sprig. Either finely chop or grind with a mortar and pestle.
- Trim the lamb shoulder of any excessive fat and cut into cubes approximately 2" in size. Season the lamb with ¾ teaspoon salt and ¼ teaspoon pepper. Place flour in a large bowl or a large, clean paper bag. Add lamb and toss to coat lamb cubes evenly in flour. (If using a paper bag, fold bag shut and shake)
- Heat a Dutch Oven (or large, heavy, ovenproof pot that has a lid) on stovetop over medium heat. Add 2 tablespoons olive oil to the pot and heat the oil. Brown the lamb cubes in batches over medium heat, being careful not to overcrowd, browning on all sides.
- Set the browned lamb aside in a bowl. Cook subsequent lamb in batches, adding olive oil as needed. Transfer the last batch of browned lamb into bowl.
- Deglaze the pot by adding wine over medium heat, scraping the bottom of pot well to release any browned bits. Pour this over the lamb that is resting in a bowl.
- Add 2 teaspoons olive oil to Dutch Oven. Add chopped onion and sauté over medium heat until just beginning to turn light brown, about 6 minutes. Add a bit of olive oil during cooking, if necessary.
- Add garlic and sauté for one minute—do not brown. Add to Dutch Oven: the lamb with wine, beef stock, red wine vinegar, carrots and rosemary. Stir.
- Place Dutch Oven on center rack in 350-degree oven and bake for 2 hours. Remove Dutch Oven from oven—it will be extremely hot—use oven mitts. Place on stovetop or a heat-proof surface. If the stew looks dry, stir in up to ¾ cup beef stock. If you don't have extra stock, add a bit of wine. Check that meat is tender and can be cut easily with a fork. If not, return to oven and bake another 20-30 minutes or until meat is tender. Taste and season with salt and/or pepper if desired.

Prayers

TRADITIONAL PRAYER

Saint Martha,

I resort to thy aid and protection.

As proof of my affection and faith,

I offer thee this light,

which I shall burn every Tuesday.

   Comfort me in all my difficulties

and through the great favors thou didst enjoy

when the Savior was lodged in thy house,

intercede for my family,

that we be provided for in our necessities.

I ask of thee, Saint Martha,

to overcome all difficulties

as thou didst overcome the dragon

which thou hadst at thy feet.

In the name of the Father

and of the Son and of the Holy Spirit.

   Amen.

CONTEMPORARY PRAYER

St. Martha, like you, I can become anxious and worried about many things. Help me to relax and trust that I do not have to be in charge of everything for it to work out. Amen.

CHAPTER 16

Bl. Solanus Casey

Solanus Casey sat on his stool and looked out the partially open front door of the cottage. The celestial sunset made him smile in gratitude. *Any moment the guest of honor should be arriving,* he thought.

Solanus was pleased to be the person chosen to watch for the first signs of arrival. When he lived on earth, some of his happiest days were spent as the porter/doorkeeper for Saint Bonaventure convent in Detroit. He hooked his heels on the lower rung of the stool and leaned against the door frame. Behind him, he could hear the rise and fall of voices, punctuated by the occasional ripple of laughter. He enjoyed a good gathering, but he took his responsibilities as the doorkeeper seriously.

When Peter invited him to the dinner party, he refused at first. "I'm not a Saint with a capital "S," he had objected. "I'm just a Blessed. Everyone else there will have been canonized."

Peter rolled his eyes. "How many times do I have to tell you that those differences aren't important up here? Venerable, Blessed, Saint . . . we don't pay any attention to the titles."

In the early church, saints could simply be named by their bishop, but over the years, the process became more formalized. Today it is a multi-step process that begins at the diocesan level. No sooner than five years after a person has died, the bishop of the place where the person is buried opens an investigation into the alleged holiness of the person in question. A thorough investigation of the person's writings, etc., is undertaken, a biography is written, and eyewitnesses are examined. If there is sufficient evidence that the person was holy, the local bishop then presents the case of the person who is now called Servant of God to the Congregation for the Causes of Saints in Rome, a Vatican department that oversees canonizations, where a postulator takes up the cause.

After extensive evidence has been gathered, the Congregation can tell the Pope that the Servant of God was "heroic" in virtue and recommend that the person can be called Venerable. While this is not a definitive decree attesting to the holiness of the person, prayers can be offered to them for a miracle, which is necessary for the next step, Beatification.

In order to be named Blessed, proof of a miracle, usually a medical cure, is required as a sign that the person is in heaven. Martyrs are an exception to this regulation because it is assumed that if the person voluntarily gave his or her life for the faith, they are in heaven.

The final step in the canonization process is the declaration of sainthood, which usually requires a second verified miracle. Very rarely in special circumstances, the need for a second miracle can waived. This happens only if the Pope, the Cardinals, and the Congregation for the Causes of Saints all agree upon the undeniable holiness of the person in question. Such was the case of Pope John XXIII in 2014. Once canonized, a saint is assigned a feast day, usually the day of his or her death—his or her birthday into heaven. If a more prominent saint already has that day or if the day is permanently assigned to a feast such as December 25 and Christmas, an alternative date may be used.

Solanus sighed. "Who is going to be there?"

"Teresa of Avila, John Henry Newman, Augustine . . . a whole group."

"Is Francis of Assisi going to be there?" Solanus asked. Peter nodded.

"I am not worthy to be with all of them," Solanus argued. "They founded religious orders—Francis founded the religious order I belonged to, for heaven's sake! They developed theology. Wrote books. They did all sorts of things. I lived in the Midwestern United States my whole life. And I was just a 'simplex priest.'"

Peter made a sort of harrumphing sound. "I wasn't exactly a regular priest myself," he muttered under his breath, then said aloud, "I think you will be glad if you come. How about if you are the doorkeeper? You can let people in and then let everyone know when the guest of honor is coming. How about that?"

Solanus smiled, and his long white beard bobbed. "That I can do. That I can do," he agreed.

"Don't forget that it's a potluck," Peter said as he left. "We all are supposed to bring something to share."

"Now you tell me," Solanus sighed, then his eyes twinkled with childlike glee. *I know what I'll do*, he thought. *I'll make my 'one bowl' special.* He chuckled at the thought.

At the party, Solanus checked the horizon. Nothing yet, he thought. Then he realized that his "one bowl" special was still in the refrigerator. He hopped off the stool and headed to the kitchen. Martha was doing the last of a pile of dishes. "Hi there," Solanus said. "I've just come to get my dessert." He pulled a heaping bowl of cereal-milk ice cream with coffee-caramel sauce from the freezer.

A "simplex priest" is a priest who is allowed to say Mass but is not usually allowed to hear confessions or preach. This restriction is generally applied to men who have had difficulties with academic studies. It does not indicate a lesser degree of priesthood, only a variance in duties.

• • • • • • • • • • • • • • • • • • •

Solanus was frequently observed by his fellow monks eating all of his breakfast at once in the same bowl. He would pour cereal, juice, coffee, and milk all together.

"You better take some ice to keep it cold," Martha said.

"No, I'm good," Solanus said, cradling the bowl in his arms. "It will be fine. It won't be long before the guest of honor arrives and besides, I have a thing for keeping ice cream cold," he added mysteriously.

"If you say so," Martha said doubtfully, as he left the kitchen.

Solanus placed his bowl next to Francis's almond cookies and Lydia's Turkish Delight with a look of satisfaction. "So, what kind of dessert did you bring?" Kateri asked as she came up beside him. "You said you brought a dessert when we talked earlier."

"Ice cream," Solanus said. "With salted orange-honey brittle. Would you like a taste?"

Kateri hesitated. "I really shouldn't. It might spoil my appetite," she said and then laughed. "I used to do everything I could to spoil my appetite on earth and I'm still thinking about it now. Maybe I don't need to do that anymore," she added, picking up a piece of the brittle. "Delicious honey taste," she exclaimed. "I used to gather honey when I was on earth."

"I kept bees when I lived in Huntington, Indiana," he said. "Lovely little town, Huntington."

Kateri licked her fingers. "A saint from Indiana. How often does that happen?"

Solanus shook his head. "Not a saint yet," he said. "Just Blessed."

Kateri shook her head in turn. "You are a saint. It just takes people on earth some time to catch up. I wasn't canonized until 2012, but I'd been up here for more than 300 years. Just give it a little more time."

Solanus smiled gently. "I can wait. Now," he said, "I suggest you go find your place at the table. I have a hunch that the guest of honor will be arriving soon."

Did You Know?

One Christmas, a friar found Solanus playing his violin and singing carols before the crèche.

BIOGRAPHY ⤝

Bl. Solanus Casey

NOVEMBER 25, 1870 – JULY 31, 1957

Solanus Casey was born Bernard Francis Casey, the sixth of sixteen children of Irish immigrants. When he was eight, he contracted diphtheria, which left his voice raspy. His family moved several times, and this limited his education. When he was eighteen, he left his family and the farm and worked a series of manual jobs, including logger, hospital orderly, prison guard in the Minnesota state prison, and a streetcar operator. His desire to be married ended when the mother of a girl to whom he proposed sent her to a boarding school.

His thoughts turned toward religious life when he saw someone assault a woman on the streetcar tracks. (Some accounts say that the woman was stabbed to death in front of him.) Deeply affected by this event, he decided to dedicate his life to God. As part of the call he felt, he wanted to become a diocesan priest, so he applied to Saint Francis High School Seminary in the Archdiocese of Milwaukee in January 1891. His application was denied because classes were taught in German and Latin, and Solanus did not speak, read, or write either of them. He was advised that he should try to join a religious order where he would not have to hear confessions or preach in public.

It is said that Solanus met some of Jesse James's companions when he was working as a prison guard.

• •

While order priests are sometimes referred to as "religious," this is not a designator of degrees of holiness. The differences between diocesan and religious or order priests are primarily how they live. Order priests typically live in a community where they eat, pray, and recreate together while diocesan priests often live alone. Another difference is that diocesan priests make promises at ordination while religious priests make solemn vows. A diocesan priest promises to obey his bishop and to live a celibate life. An order priest, in a solemn religious ceremony (hence the name religious), vows to live in poverty, meaning he will share his goods with the community; in chastity, meaning he will be celibate; and in obedience to his superiors with regard to everything from his residence to his schedules.

Uncertain of his next step, he prayed before a statue of the Virgin and heard her voice telling him, "Go to Detroit." He took this to mean he should apply to the Order of Friars Minor Capuchin there. He did so and was accepted on January 14, 1897.

The Orders of Friar Minor Capuchin is one of three current branches of religious in the Franciscan Order founded by Francis of Assisi. In addition to the Friars Minor Capuchin (Capuchins), there are the Friars Minor (Franciscans), and the Conventuals (Minorites). Divisions in the Franciscan Order based on how the friars thought they should live developed almost immediately after the death of Francis, and they continue to this day.

• •

Solanus loved to play his violin and sing, but his singing voice was so horrible other friars found it difficult to listen. Once when a friar was sick, Solanus offered to sing for him. While he was getting his violin, the sick friar asked another visitor to turn on the radio to prevent Solanus from singing when he returned. When his fellow friars didn't want to listen to him, he would sometimes play before the Blessed Sacrament in the chapel.

Despite his struggles with his academic studies, his obvious faith convinced his superiors to allow him to be ordained a simplex priest in 1904. He celebrated his first Mass in Appleton, Wisconsin, with many of his family present. For the next two decades, he was assigned to various friaries in New York, including in Yonkers, the Lower East Side, and Harlem, where he became well known for his insights, compassion, and overall holiness.

When he was transferred to Saint Bonaventure's in Detroit in 1924, his real life work began. While serving primarily as a receptionist and doorkeeper for the next twenty years, he came in contact with thousands of people who came seeking his prayers and advice both day and night. His reputation as a possible miracle worker brought the ill, the suffering, and the desperate to him in a steady stream. When he wasn't occupied with his duties, he would kneel for hours in prayer before the Eucharist at night. He also helped found the Capuchin Soup Kitchen, which still operates today.

In 1946, when his health began to falter, he was moved to Huntington, Indiana, the home of the novitiate of Saint Felix. There he lived a quiet, reserved life. In 1957, after hospitalization for food poisoning, he was diagnosed with erysipelas, an ulcerative skin disease. It was so bad, doctors thought about amputating his leg, but he rallied until the summer when he was taken to the hospital for the last time. One of his sisters came to visit him, but he died at Saint John Hospital in Detroit on July 31, with only a nurse in attendance. It was said that his last words were, "I give my soul to Jesus Christ."

More than 20,000 people attended his funeral and more than 70,000 his beatification Mass on November 18, 2017, at Ford Field in Detroit. His miracle for beatification was the 2012 cure of Paula Medina Zarate's ichthyosis, the same skin condition that ultimately led to his death.

Legends, Lore, and Miracles

Fr. Tom Nguyen, OFM CAP., a Capuchin friar who lives in Detroit, tells the story that on a summer day in 1941, a novice came to see Fr. Solanus because of a toothache. If the dentist couldn't fix the problem quickly, the novice would be sent home. Solanus told him to go to the dentist and trust God. In the meantime, a visitor brought Solanus two ice cream cones. Despite his secretary's consternation, Solanus put them in a desk drawer. When the novice returned more than a half an hour later, with a miraculously healthy tooth, Solanus reached in the drawer and pulled out three (not two) perfectly intact ice cream cones, which he shared with the novice and his secretary.

Fr. Solanus had a special rapport with bees. Father Benedict Groeschel, cofounder of the Franciscan Friars of the Renewal, was once caught in a swarm of angry bees while visiting St. Felix Friary in Huntington. Fr. Solanus soon arrived and began talking to the bees. Fr. Groeschel recalled in an interview for the *Our Sunday Visitor* newspaper that Fr. Solanus said, "All right now. Calm down. All right." The bees immediately calmed down and returned to their hive. Fr. Groeschel added that when Solanus realized that there were two queen bees in the hive, he stuck his bare hand in the hive and pulled out the second queen without being stung. Others noted that he sometimes calmed bees by playing his harmonica.

By 1966, reports of twenty-four major cures were attributed to Solanus after his death, even though his cause for canonization was not formally opened until 1982. One unverified case involved a volunteer at the soup kitchen Solanus helped found. The man was being rolled into the operating room for the removal of a stomach tumor. Solanus put his hand on the man's stomach and told him to have the doctors make one last check before cutting. They did and the tumor had vanished.

Quote
"Give thanks ahead of time."

Recipe

——◆——

Cereal-Milk Ice Cream with Coffee-Caramel Sauce and Salted Orange-Honey Brittle

This custard ice cream recipe is a tribute to Solanus's breakfast-in-a-bowl, as well as the miracle of the ice cream and his care for bees.

- **PREP TIME:** 15 minutes
- **COOK TIME:** 50 minutes, plus chill time of 4-5 hours, plus churn time
- **YIELD:** 8-10 servings
- **SPECIAL EQUIPMENT:** Helpful: Candy thermometer and ice cream maker
- **MAKE IT LACTO-OVO VEGAN:** Use a Vegan Corn Flake cereal. If you don't consume honey, substitute with corn syrup or agave syrup.
- **MAKE IT GLUTEN-FREE:** Use Corn Flakes and Instant Coffee labeled as Gluten-Free. As always, ensure that all ingredients you cook with are gluten-free.

Custard Ice Cream

——◆——

INGREDIENTS

3 cups corn flakes cereal	2 tablespoons light corn syrup
2½ cups heavy cream	1 tablespoon honey
3½ cups milk (not low-fat)	Pinch salt
1 cup sugar	6 egg yolks

DIRECTIONS

Note: If using an ice cream maker, you may need to freeze your canister the day before.

- In a large saucepan: add cereal, cream, and milk. Stir well to combine. Cover and cook over medium-low heat for 20 minutes, stirring occasionally.
- Have ready a large bowl and mesh strainer. Pour the contents of saucepan through strainer into bowl. Push the cereal into the strainer to release as much liquid as you can. Discard wet cereal or use for another purpose, such as adding to muffins.
- Return cream/milk mixture to saucepan over medium-low heat. Add the sugar, corn syrup, honey, and salt. Stir to combine. Cook until sugar is dissolved, stirring occasionally.

- Whisk egg yolks in medium bowl. Begin tempering the eggs by adding ¼ cup of the hot milk/cream to the eggs while whisking. Continue 4 more additions of hot milk and cream, ¼ cup at a time, whisking constantly to avoid curdling the eggs.
- Pour the egg/milk/cream mixture into the saucepan. Attach a candy thermometer to side of saucepan. Cook over low heat, stirring constantly: you do not want the eggs to solidify into scrambled eggs. Cook until the mixture measures 175 degrees Fahrenheit on your candy thermometer, about 15-20 minutes. When it's done you should be able to dip a spoon into the hot mixture, and the mixture will coat the back of the spoon—and when you run your finger through the mixture on the back of the spoon, a line in the middle remains without the custard running (the line you drew with your finger holds its shape).
- Strain the mixture through a fine-mesh sieve into a heatproof bowl. Cover and refrigerate at least 4 hours or overnight.
- Once it is chilled, process the mixture in your ice cream maker.

If you don't have an ice cream maker:
- Pour the chilled ice cream mixture into a large mixing bowl, cover with plastic wrap and place in freezer. After a few hours, remove from freezer and mix with electric mixer for a few minutes, scraping sides with spatula. Return to freezer for 90 minutes. Repeat this mixing process and return to freezer. Continue repeating this process until it is like soft-serve ice cream.
- Or: Place chilled mixture in a gallon freezer bag that can zip closed. Freeze for a few hours. Then every 60-90 minutes, take the bag out and vigorously squeeze the bag to break up ice crystals and combine them with the unfrozen portions.

Coffee-Caramel Sauce

- **PREP TIME:** 5 minutes
- **COOK TIME:** 5-6 minutes
- **YIELD:** 1¼ Cups Sauce

INGREDIENTS

5 tablespoons butter	⅓ cup half and half
1 cup packed brown sugar	4 tablespoons espresso powder or instant coffee
1 tablespoon corn syrup	pinch of salt

DIRECTIONS

• Melt butter in medium-sized sauté pan over medium-high heat. Add all other ingredients, stir to combine. Cook until bubbly, stirring constantly. Then continue to cook (it should be bubbling/boiling) for 90 seconds to 2 minutes. Remove pan from heat and pour hot sauce into a heatproof serving container.

Orange-Honey Brittle with Sea Salt

• **PREP TIME:** 4 minutes
• **COOK TIME:** 6 minutes
• **YIELD:** About ½ cup brittle

INGREDIENTS

2 tablespoons butter

¼ cup packed brown sugar

1 tablespoon honey

1 heaping teaspoon orange zest

1 tablespoon fresh-squeezed orange juice

½ cup corn flakes, crushed

Sea salt

DIRECTIONS

Prepare a baking sheet lightly coated with oil or sprayed with non-stick cooking spray.

• In medium sauté pan, melt butter. Add brown sugar, honey, orange juice, and orange zest. Stir well. Cook over medium-high heat without stirring for 4-5 minutes until it turns to a caramel consistency and begins to darken. Remove from heat and add crushed corn flakes, stirring them in immediately to combine. Spread out immediately onto oiled cookie sheet and sprinkle with a bit of sea salt while still hot. Allow to cool and harden. Break up pieces to use as topping for this ice cream sundae. (It also makes a nice candy.)

• Serve: Scoop ice cream into a bowl, pour warm coffee caramel syrup over the ice cream, and top with pieces of orange-honey brittle.

Prayers

TRADITIONAL PRAYER

CANONIZATION PRAYER:

O God, I adore You. I give myself to You.
 May I be the person You want me to be,
and May Your will be done in my life today.
I thank You for the gifts You gave Father Solanus.
If it is Your Will, bless us with the Canonization of
Father Solanus so that others may imitate
and carry on his love for all the poor and
suffering of our world.
As he joyfully accepted Your divine plans,
I ask You, according to Your Will,
to hear my prayer for . . . (your intention)
through Jesus Christ our Lord. Amen.
"Blessed be God in all His Designs."

CONTEMPORARY PRAYER

B lessed Fr. Casey, help me to be grateful no matter what happens to me and
 teach me to see the hand of the Divine touching me throughout my life.
Amen.

CONCLUSION

Guests of Honor

WITH ONE FINAL RECIPE

A glimmer of gold shone on the horizon. "They're coming," Solanus called out as hopped off his stool. He hurried through the room calling out breathlessly, "They're coming. They're coming." Opening the back door, he announced in his raspy voice, "It's time, come on!" to the women who were still sitting under the grape arbor.

The gathering of saints clustered around the front door. In the distance, the golden glow could be seen drawing ever closer. A small group, led by St. Peter and flanked by several angels, their wings sparkling as if they were dusted with diamonds, walked up the path. In the middle of the group, looking rather stunned and confused, were a husband and wife.

"We're here!" St. Peter announced, and then stepped aside to let the couple enter.

The man peered cautiously inside the cottage and then gasped at the sight of the saints, the buffet table, and the head table. "Where are we?" he whispered to his wife. She shook her head and glanced nervously around.

"Well, what are you waiting for?" Peter encouraged. "Go on in. Everyone's waiting for you."

The woman stepped forward, and the room broke into applause. She looked over her shoulder at her husband, who gave a sort of helpless shrug. Peter led them to the head table, where their names suddenly appeared in gold letters on the name cards. The woman reached out to touch hers, then pulled her hand back and looked questioningly at Peter. "Sit down," Peter said. "This is where you belong." He pulled out the chair for the woman, and she gingerly sat down. Her husband sat down next to her and looked silently around the room. Suddenly he nudged his wife and whispered, "Look over there, at the door." She looked where he was pointing. "I think that's Blessed Solanus Casey," he said excitedly.

"I think you're right," she said. "I asked him to protect us when, well, when *it* happened. I wonder if he heard my prayer?"

Just then, Solanus looked at them and gave a little wink and a thumbs up. "I'm pretty sure he did," the husband said, as the kitchen door opened and a flash of blinding white light filled the room. Joshua ben Joseph, better known as Jesus of Nazareth, approached the table. "My Lord," the man whispered in astonishment as he tried to stand. His wife attempted to kneel, but the tablecloth got in her way.

"Stay," Jesus said. "I am just here to tell you how very glad we all are that you have arrived. We've all been watching you and could hardly wait to meet you, our newest saints."

"Saints?" the husband said. "We aren't saints. I'm just a grocery store manager."

"And I am, *was*, a kindergarten teacher," added the wife.

"Ah," Jesus said, "but you are saints, great saints."

"I don't understand," the wife said, pushing from her forehead a strand of hair that was still damp from the tsunami. "We didn't do anything special like these people did." She pointed to the heavenly assembly.

"When the tidal wave came, we weren't helping the poor or anything. We were just on vacation," her husband added.

"Do you remember that little boy who never had a clean shirt?" Jesus turned toward the woman. "You bought him two new ones and you used to take the dirty ones home and wash them."

"Yes," the woman said. "He was ashamed that he didn't have clean clothes."

"Because of what you did, he didn't become a drug addict like his mother," Jesus said. "He will go on to graduate from community college and become a successful plumber." He turned to the husband, "Do you remember how you used to take the blemished produce to the food bank?" The husband nodded. "You made sure that countless hungry families had fresh fruit and vegetables."

"But I didn't always go to church on Sunday," the husband protested. "And I didn't read the Bible or pray all the time."

"And I yelled at our kids and I never liked to pray the Rosary," the woman added. "How can we be saints?"

"Did you love?" Jesus asked, his voice growing soft.

The husband took his wife's hand. "We tried," he said. "We tried our best." His wife nodded in agreement.

"But now these three remain: faith, hope, and love. But the greatest of these is love," Jesus said. "Love is what makes saints. It's the only thing that does."

"Can we get this party started?" A voice that sounded suspiciously like Brigit's came from the back of the room near the wine jars.

"My soup is getting cold," Augustine said. "Let's eat!" Other voices murmured in agreement.

Jesus picked up the wife's plate. "What can I get you?" he asked.

"Oh no, my Lord, it is I who should be serving you," she protested.

"Forget it," Peter said, leaning in. "I tried that at the Last Supper. He won't hear of it."

Jesus smiled fondly and then added, "I would suggest you try the roast locusts. My relative John brought them, and he says they are his best batch ever."

One Last Recipe!

Roast Locusts

While you could try to capture your own grasshoppers or locusts, they are available online and in some specialty grocery stores.

- **PREP TIME** 5 minutes
- **COOK TIME:** 5 to 6 minutes total

INGREDIENTS

About 25 locusts

10 cups of vegetable stock or lightly salted water

Sea salt

Olive oil

DIRECTIONS

- Bring stock or water to a boil. Toss locusts in boiling stock. Cook for 3 minutes.
- Drain the locusts and let them cool.
- Remove wings. Heads and small legs may also be removed.
- Fry in olive oil for 1½-2 minutes, until browned.
- Toss with sea salt to taste.
- Attempt to eat.

1 Ordinary of Saint-Jean-Longueuil, 740 Boulevard Sainte-Foy, Longueuil, QC J4J 1Z3, Canada

2 USCCB United States Conference of Catholic Bishops Migration and Refugee Service https://www.usccb.org/about/migration-and-refugee-services/national-migration-week /upload/M7-266-Josephine-Bakhita-Prayer-Card.pdf https://www.usccb.org/

3 USCCB General Instruction of the Roman Missal https://www.usccb.org/prayer-and -worship/the-mass/general-instruction-of-the-roman-missal

4 *The Roman Missal*: Common of Holy Men and Women—For a Holy Woman https://www .usccb.org/prayer-and-worship/the-mass/general-instruction-of-the-roman-missal

Who We Are

As the publishing arm of the Community of Jesus, Paraclete Press presents a full expression of Christian belief and practice—from Catholic to Evangelical, from Protestant to Orthodox, reflecting the ecumenical charism of the Community and its dedication to sacred music, the fine arts, and the written word. We publish books, recordings, sheet music, and video/DVDs that nourish the vibrant life of the church and its people.

What We Are Doing

BOOKS | PARACLETE PRESS BOOKS show the richness and depth of what it means to be Christian. While Benedictine spirituality is at the heart of who we are and all that we do, our books reflect the Christian experience across many cultures, time periods, and houses of worship.

We have many series, including *Paraclete Essentials*; *Paraclete Fiction*; *Paraclete Poetry*; *Paraclete Giants*; and for children and adults, *All God's Creatures*, books about animals and faith; and *San Damiano Books*, focusing on Franciscan spirituality. Others include *Voices from the Monastery* (men and women monastics writing about living a spiritual life today), *Active Prayer*, and new for young readers: *The Pope's Cat*. We also specialize in gift books for children on the occasions of Baptism and First Communion, as well as other important times in a child's life, and books that bring creativity and liveliness to any adult spiritual life.

The MOUNT TABOR BOOKS series focuses on the arts and literature as well as liturgical worship and spirituality; it was created in conjunction with the Mount Tabor Ecumenical Centre for Art and Spirituality in Barga, Italy.

MUSIC | PARACLETE PRESS DISTRIBUTES RECORDINGS of the internationally acclaimed choir *Gloriæ Dei Cantores*, the *Gloriæ Dei Cantores Schola*, and the other instrumental artists of the *Arts Empowering Life Foundation*.

PARACLETE PRESS IS THE EXCLUSIVE NORTH AMERICAN DISTRIBUTOR for the Gregorian chant recordings from St. Peter's Abbey in Solesmes, France. Paraclete also carries all of the Solesmes chant publications for Mass and the Divine Office, as well as their academic research publications.

In addition, PARACLETE PRESS SHEET MUSIC publishes the work of today's finest composers of sacred choral music, annually reviewing over 1,000 works and releasing between 40 and 60 works for both choir and organ.

VIDEO | Our video/DVDs offer spiritual help, healing, and biblical guidance for a broad range of life issues including grief and loss, marriage, forgiveness, facing death, understanding suicide, bullying, addictions, Alzheimer's, and Christian formation.

Learn more about us at our website:
www.paracletepress.com
or phone us toll-free at 1.800.451.5006

SCAN
TO
READ

You may also be interested in these . . .

Saints at Heart
How Fault-Filled, Problem-Prone, Imperfect People Like Us Can Be Holy

Bert Ghezzi

ISBN 978-1-64060-203-8 | Trade paperback | $14.99